THE LAWS AND LIBERTIES
OF MASSACHUSETTS

THE LAWS AND LIBERTIES OF MASSACHUSETTS

REPRINTED FROM THE
UNIQUE COPY OF THE 1648 EDITION
IN THE HENRY E. HUNTINGTON LIBRARY

With an Introduction by
RICHARD S. DUNN

THE HUNTINGTON LIBRARY
SAN MARINO · CALIFORNIA

LIBRARY OF CONGRESS CATALOGING-IN-PUBLICATION DATA

Massachusetts (Colony)
[Laws, statutes, etc.]
The laws and liberties of Massachusetts : reprinted from the copy of the 1648 edition
in the Henry E. Huntington Library / with an introduction by Richard S. Dunn.
p.   cm.
Rev. ed. of: The book of the general lawes and libertyes concerning
the inhabitants of the Massachusets. Facsim. ed.
Cambridge, Mass. : Harvard University Press, 1929.
"The present edition, a reprint of 1929 type facsimile, commemorates
the 350th anniversary of publication of this remarkable volume"—Introd.
ISBN 0-87328-173-x (alk. paper)
1. Law—Massachusetts.   I. Henry E. Huntington Library and Art Gallery.
II. Massachusetts (Colony).   Book of the general lawes and libertyes concerning the
inhabitants of the Massachusets.   III. Title.
KFM2430 1648.A43   98-8646
348.744´022—dc21   CIP

INTRODUCTION

*T*HE *BOOK of the General Lawes and Libertyes concerning the Inhabitants of the Massachusets* is the first compilation of laws and constitutional rights to be printed in English America, and it is arguably the most important statement of political, religious, and economic freedoms and obligations ever issued in the colonial era. As the title page states, the Massachusetts General Court authorized the publication of this book when the court convened at Boston on the fourteenth of the first month 1647—March 14, 1648, in the modern calendar. The court ordered that six hundred copies be printed in Cambridge (where Stephen Day operated New England's only printing press), and then sold in Hezekiah Usher's Boston bookshop at three shillings each, with fifty copies given free of charge to the magistrates and deputies who sat in the court. By 1651, when most copies had already been distributed, the remaining stock was destroyed because the General Court had passed new legislation that invalidated portions of the 1648 text. In 1660 and again in 1672 new revised law books were published that superseded the 1648 edition. By the nineteenth century, not a single copy of the 1648 book could be found. When William Whitmore produced a documentary collection of seventeenth-century Massachusetts laws in 1890, he had to omit the 1648 compilation. But shortly afterward a copy surfaced in England, and this unique copy was subsequently acquired by the Huntington Library. In 1929 the Huntington produced a line-by-line type facsimile edition (published by Harvard University Press), and in 1975 the Huntington produced a photographic facsimile edition. The present edition, a reprint of the 1929 type facsimile, commemorates the 350th anniversary of publication of this remarkable volume.

By 1648 the Massachusetts magistrates and deputies had been debating for more than a dozen years whether to frame a body of laws—and if so, how to accomplish the task. At first, from 1630 to 1634, the colony magistrates under the leadership of Governor John Winthrop had made all the administrative, legislative, and judicial decisions, and had exercised very free discretionary authority. But once the magistrates agreed in 1634 to share taxing and legislative power with deputies from each of the colony's towns, there was pressure within the General Court to create a comprehensive set of fundamental laws that would bind and limit the magistrates. A committee was appointed in 1635 to draft a code "in resemblance to a Magna Carta," and further committees were appointed in 1636 and 1638; little was accomplished, however, since the magistrates who sat on these committees wished to preserve their administrative and judicial independence. "The people had long desired a body of laws," Winthrop noted in his journal in 1639, "and thought their condition very unsafe, while so much power rested in the discretion of magistrates." But Winthrop went on to explain that most of the magistrates thought the colonists were not yet well enough settled in their beliefs and behavior to fix upon a binding set of fundamental rules, and that it was much better "to raise up laws by practice and custom" as had been done in England for many centuries.

In 1636 John Cotton, the leading minister in the colony, submitted a draft law code to the General Court. This code was variously called "a modell of the Iudiciall lawes of Moses" or "a model of Moses his judicials." As both titles indicate, Cotton was attempting to establish rules for the people of Massachusetts analogous to Moses' rules for the Israelites. Winthrop found this Old Testament system far too restrictive, and he particularly objected to Cotton's borrowing from Exodus and Leviticus to impose mandatory death sentences on persons found guilty of adultery, incest, sodomy, reviling the magistrates, or profaning the Sabbath. Cotton's model was not accepted by the Massachusetts government, probably because the other colony leaders agreed with Winthrop that the design was too rigid, as well as too brief and incomplete. But elements of Cotton's Mosaic draft were incorporated into the Massachusetts codes of 1641 and 1648, and the founders of New Haven Colony adopted his framework when they drew up the first set of laws for their colony.

In 1638 or 1639 Nathaniel Ward presented a second and very different model, known as "The Body of Liberties." This code was circulated to all the towns for comment, was revised by the General Court, and was finally adopted provisionally in 1641 for a three-year trial period. As the prefatory Epistle to *The Book of the General Lawes and Libertyes* explains, Ward's code was not construed in 1641 as fundamental law, and perhaps for this reason the court "published" it by circulating manuscript copies rather than having it printed in Cambridge. Fortunately one of these manuscript copies has survived. It consists of one hundred clauses, of which eighty-six were retained seven years later in the *Lawes and Libertyes*. Nonetheless, the 1641 text is strikingly different in character from the 1648 text. The Body of Liberties, as its name implies, is primarily a bill of rights. The great majority of the clauses enumerate the "freedomes" and "priveledges" belonging to the inhabitants of Massachusetts that safeguard them from arbitrary government. These include basic civil liberties (seventeen clauses), judicial liberties (thirty-one clauses), the liberties of freemen (seven clauses), "Liberties of Woemen" (two clauses), "Liberties of Children" (four clauses), "Liberties of Servants" (four clauses), and "Liberties of Forreiners and Strangers" (three clauses). The liberties of the churches are articulated with special elaboration, and twelve capital crimes—taken from Cotton's Mosaic code—are also appended.

John Winthrop cannot have been satisfied with the thrust of the Body of Liberties, because he believed—as he told the General Court in 1645—that the inhabitants of Massachusetts were too fond of their freedom and too rebellious against their elected leaders. The people, in his view, have liberty only to do that which is good, just, and honest, and Christian freedom requires discipline and submission to governmental authority. Winthrop's critics, for their part, also had reason to press for further fundamental laws, because the Body of Liberties did little if anything to limit the discretionary power of the magistrates in administrative affairs. This became obvious in 1645 when the magistrates ordered the Hingham militia company to accept a captain who was not their choice, and the people of Hingham protested en masse to the General Court. The deputies adopted Hingham's cause and staged an impeachment trial of Winthrop. The quarrel was papered over and Winthrop was exonerated, but the deputies retained their basic distrust of executive independence. Yet in the aftermath of the Hingham fracas the magistrates began to agree with the deputies about the need for a more comprehensive code of fundamental laws. This was mainly because by the mid-1640s the people of Massachusetts had settled into a political and religious culture that differed distinctly from what their fellow Puritans were trying to establish in England, and—much closer at hand—from what the radical Puritans who had been expelled from the Bay Colony in the 1630s had created in neighboring Rhode Island. Magistrates and deputies could agree that all incendiary religious deviants must be kept out of Massachusetts, and that all agitators for such dangerous new ideas as religious toleration must be silenced. And to validate these policies they needed a law code that articulated in full detail their particular form of government.

In 1646 and 1647 the General Court united almost unanimously against a group of seven men known as the Remonstrants, who claimed that the Massachusetts government denied them their civil and religious rights as Englishmen. When the Remonstrants dared to appeal to Parliament for protection, the court sentenced them to jail and fined them savagely. The Remonstrants had argued that the Massachusetts Bay Company was a corporation with limited powers, not a free state, and that the liberties of the colonists were endangered because the General Court rejected English law and drew up inadequate, ill-framed laws in substitution. The court drew heavily upon the Body of Liberties in refuting the Remonstrants, but saw the need for a fuller printed codification. So the Remonstrants' challenge accelerated the push for a book that combined guarantees of individual liberty with statutes delineating community governance. The court enacted many new laws in 1646 and 1647 to fill gaps in the existing code, and one of the leading committee members, Joseph Hills (speaker of the house of deputies), reported that he combed through English statute books looking for laws that might be suitable for Massachusetts. Publication of the *General Lawes and Libertyes* was authorized, as we have noted, in March 1648, and last-minute changes were ordered in May 1648 when the book was in press at Cambridge.

A brief analysis of the contents of this book will demonstrate its breadth and significance. The 1648 text is over four times as long as the 1641 Body of Liberties. It incorporates and elaborates upon almost all of the provisions from 1641; and it adds over two hundred laws enacted by the General Court during 1630–1640 and

1642–1647. The book purposely omits, however, a great deal of nonstatutory or common law that was in force in Massachusetts in 1648. The General Court describes the compilation as "general" law as distinguished from civil or "private" law: it contains few provisions concerning contract, property transactions, defamation, or trespass, and no mention is made of probate of wills. The volume is organized topically "into an Alphabetical order" in imitation of English legal handbooks such as Michael Dalton's *Countrey Justice*, moving from a definition of "Abilitie" on page 1 to a court order on "Wrecks of the sea" on page 55. For example, under the heading "Charges publick" on pages 9–11, eight laws passed between 1634 and 1647 that stipulate how to collect and disburse money and how to recruit labor for public purposes are grouped into four subdivisions. Each law is dated [within brackets], and all laws dated [1641] are from the Body of Liberties. However, because of the alphabetical arrangement, the "liberties" enumerated collectively in 1641 are now scattered throughout the book. A table of contents was added at the end, but it is missing from the Huntington copy.

King Charles I, who had granted a royal charter to the Massachusetts Bay Company in 1629, was a prisoner of Parliament in 1648 and was to be executed the next year. The king is not mentioned anywhere in the *General Lawes and Libertyes*, and Parliament is referred to only in the prefatory Epistle. Nor is there any statement of allegiance to the English state. The General Court assumes, without saying so, that it is self-sufficient and autonomous. And the citation from Paul's Epistle to the Romans on the title page affirms the colony's dedication to the service of God. The prefatory Epistle from the General Court to "our beloved brethren and neighbours the Inhabitants of the Massachusets" emphasizes—as John Cotton had done in his Mosaic code—the parallel between God's chosen people in Israel and in New England, as well as the union of church and state in both places. The biblical and moral construction placed upon social relations is evident throughout. The capital laws enumerated on pages 5–6 (which are taken from Cotton's code) impose the death penalty for idolatry, witchcraft, blasphemy, bestiality, sodomy, and adultery, in addition to murder and treason. Children above the age of sixteen who curse or smite or rebel against their parents are likewise to be executed. Heretics, Jesuits, and Anabaptists, however, are merely to be banished (pages 24, 26, 2). Taverns are closely regulated and drunkards heavily fined (pages 29–31); profane swearers are put in the stocks (page 45); and sinful games like shuffleboard are prohibited (page 24).

The ecclesiastical laws grouped on pages 18–20 spell out the terms of union between church and state in Massachusetts—which are quite different from church-state relations in England. Churches are gathered independently by "people of God" who covenant together, but each new church fellowship must be validated by the magistrates and the neighboring clergy to make sure that "the rules of Christ" are followed. All inhabitants (including those who are not members of a church) are required to attend religious services and to pay church taxes. All churches in good standing have full liberty to elect their officers (including clergy) and to admit, censure, or expel their members. And only church members in good standing are eligible to become freemen.

Complementing this exacting and overtly Puritanical religious culture is a strenuous insistence upon individual human rights and obligations. The preamble and opening declaration on page 1 are both taken from the Body of Liberties, and they frame the *Lawes and Libertyes* with the guarantee that life, liberty, and property in Massachusetts are always protected under the law. But the people who enjoy these personal freedoms are also required to participate actively in community affairs. Provisions detailing the rights and duties of freemen (pages 16–17, 21–22, 23), the governance of towns (pages 4, 6–8, 9–11, 13, 25, 35, 50–51), the regulation of militia companies (pages 39–43), the powers of juries (pages 31–32), and the institution of schools (page 47) all illustrate how the people of Massachusetts are expected to share communal burdens and to cooperate with their local leaders and neighbors.

In sum, *The Book of the General Lawes and Libertyes* admirably synthesizes the complex religious and political culture of the Bay commonwealth. Together with the Cambridge Platform of Church Discipline, which was drawn up in the very same year, 1648, by the colony clergy, the *Lawes and Libertyes* articulates an astonishingly comprehensive civil and ecclesiastical policy for such a young society. Two subsequent editions, published in 1660 and 1672, added many new entries without altering the structure and character of the 1648 text. The edition of 1672 is three times the length of the 1648 edition, but it still goes from "Ability" to "Wrecks" with an entry for "Writs" tagged on at the end. Finally, it should be stressed that the *Lawes and Libertyes* is not designed for the exclusive use of magistrates, selectmen, and clerks. This is a book for the people. The General Court directly addresses the inhabitants of Massachusetts in the prefatory Epistle, acknowledging "your longing expectation, and frequent complaints for want of such a volume to be published in print." Now that the court has finally assembled and published all recorded laws and orders that it considers of general concern, it calls upon the people—including the non-freemen, who are excluded from active participation in government—to make sure that these wholesome laws are executed. And the court urges "our beloved brethren and neighbours" to study the code closely, because if this is done, "(upon every occasion) you [may] readily see the rule which you ought to walke by."

RICHARD S. DUNN
University of Pennsylvania

FACSIMILE OF THE 1929 REPRINT

THE
BOOK OF THE GENERAL

LAUUES AND LIBERTYES

CONCERNING THE INHABITANTS OF THE MASSACHUSETS
*COLLECTED OUT OF THE RECORDS OF THE GENERAL COURT
FOR THE SEVERAL YEARS WHERIN THEY WERE MADE
AND ESTABLISHED,*

And now revised by the same Court and disposed into an Alphabetical order
and published by the same Authorit.e in the General Court
held at *Boston* the fourteenth of the
first month *Anno*
1647.

*Whosoever therefore resisteth the power, resisteth the ordinance of God,
and they that resist receive to themselves damnation.* Romanes 13. 2.

CAMBRIDGE.
Printed according to order of the GENERAL COURT.
1648.

And are to be solde at the shop of *Hezekiah Usher*
in *Boston.*

THE
BOOK OF THE GENERAL

LAUUES AND LIBERTYES

CONCERNING THE INHABITANTS OF THE MASSACHUSETS

COLLECTED OUT OF THE RECORDS OF THE GENERAL COURT
FOR THE SEVERAL YEARS WHERIN THEY WERE MADE
AND ESTABLISHED,

And now revifed by the fame Court and difpofed into an Alphabetical order
and publifhed by the fame Authoritie in the General Court
held at *Bofton* the fourteenth of the
firft month *Anno*
1 6 4 7.

VVhofoever therefore refifteth the power, refifteth the ordinance of God,
and they that refift receive to themfelves damnation. *Romanes* 13.2.

CAMBRIDGE.
Printed according to order of the *GENERAL COURT.*
1 6 4 8.

And are to be folde at the fhop of *Hezekiah Ufher*
in *Bofton*

TO OUR BELOVED BRETHREN AND NEIGHBOURS
the Inhabitants of the Maſſachuſets, the Governour, Aſſiſtants
and Deputies aſſembled in the Generall Court of that
Juriſdiction wiſh grace and peace in our
Lord Jeſus Chriſt.

S *O ſoon as God had ſet up Politicall Government among his people Iſrael hee gave
them a body of lawes for judgement both in civil and criminal cauſes. Theſe were
breif and fundamental principles, yet withall ſo full and comprehenſive as out of
them clear deductions were to be drawne to all particular caſes in future times.
For a Common-wealth without lawes is like a Ship without rigging and ſteeradge. Nor is it
ſufficient to have principles or fundamentalls, but theſe are to be drawn out into ſo many of their
deductions as the time and condition of that people may have uſe of. And it is very unſafe &
injurious to the body of the people to put them to learn their duty and libertie from generall rules,
nor is it enough to have lawes except they be alſo juſt. Therefore among other priviledges
which the Lord beſtowed upon his peculiar people, theſe he calls them ſpecially to conſider of, that
God was neerer to them and their lawes were more righteous then other nations. God was ſayd
to be amongſt them or neer to them becauſe of his Ordnances eſtabliſhed by himſelfe, and their
lawes righteous becauſe himſelfe was their Law-giver: yet in the compariſon are implyed two
things, firſt that other nations had ſomthing of Gods preſence amongſt them. Secondly that
there was alſo ſomwhat of equitie in their lawes, for it pleaſed the Father (upon the Covenant of
Redemption with his Son) to reſtore ſo much of his Image to loſt man as whereby all nations are
diſpoſed to worſhip God, and to advance righteouſnes: which appears in that of the Apoſtle*
Rom. 1. 21. They knew God &c: *and in the* 2. 14. They did by nature the things
conteined in the law of God. *But the nations corrupting his Ordinances (both of Religion,
and Juſtice) God withdrew his preſence from them proportionably whereby they were given up
to abominable luſts* Rom.2. 21. *Wheras if they had vvalked according to that light & lavv
of nature they might have been preſerved from ſuch moral evils and might have injoyed a common bleſſing in all their natural and civil Ordinances: now, if it might have been ſo with the
nations who were ſo much ſtrangers to the Covenant of Grace, what advantage bave they who
have intereſt in this Covenant, and may injoye the ſpecial preſence of God in the puritie and native ſimplicitie of all his Ordinances by which he is ſo neer to his owne people. This hath been
no ſmall priviledge, and advantage to us in New-England that our Churches, and civil State
have been planted, and growne up (like two twinnes) together like that of Iſrael in the wilder-
nes by which wee were put in minde (and had opportunitie put into our hands) not only to gather
our Churches, and ſet up the Ordinances of Chriſt Jeſus in them according to the Apoſtolick
patterne by ſuch light as the Lord graciouſly afforded us: but alſo withall to frame our civil Politie, and lawes according to the rules of his moſt holy word whereby each do help and ſtrengthen
other (the Churches the civil Authoritie, and the civil Authoritie the Churches) and ſo both
proſper the better without ſuch æmulation, and contention for priviledges or priority as have
proved the miſery (if not ruine) of both in ſome other places.
For this end about nine years ſince wee uſed the help of ſome of the Elders of our Churches
to compoſe a modell of the Iudiciall lawes of Moſes with ſuch other caſes as might be referred to
them, with intent to make uſe of them in compoſing our lawes, but not to have them publiſhed
as the lawes of this Juriſdiction: nor were they voted in Court. For that book intitled* The
Liberties &c: *publiſhed about ſeven years ſince (which conteines alſo many lawes and orders
both for civil & criminal cauſes, and is commonly (though without ground) reported to be our
Fundamentalls that wee owne as eſtabliſhed by Authoritie of this Court, and that after three
years experience & generall approbation: and accordingly we have inſerted them into this volume under the ſeverall heads to which they belong yet not as fundamentalls, for divers of them
have ſince been repealed, or altered, and more may juſtly be (at leaſt) amended heerafter as further experience ſhall diſcover defects or inconveniences for* Nihil ſimul natum et perfectum.

A 2. *The*

The fame muft we fay of this prefent Volume, we have not publifhed it as a perfect body of laws sufficient to carry on the Government eftablifhed for future times, nor could it be expected that we fhould promife fuch a thing. For if it be no difparagement to the wifedome of that High Court of Parliament in England that in four hundred years they could not fo compile their lawes, and regulate proceedings in Courts of juftice &c: but that they had ftill new work to do of the fame kinde almoft every Parliament: there can be no juft caufe to blame a poor Colonie (being unfurnifhed of Lawyers and Statefmen) that in eighteen years hath produced no more, nor better rules for a good, and fetled Government then this Book holds forth: nor have you (our Bretheren and Neighbours) any caufe, whether you look back upon our Native Country, or take your obfervation by other States, & Common wealths in Europe) to complaine of fuch as you have imployed in this fervice; for the time which hath been fpent in making lawes, and repealing and altering them fo often, nor of the charge which the Country hath been put to for thofe occafions, the Civilian gives you a fatisfactorie reafon of fuch continuall alterations additions &c: Crefcit in Orbe dolus.

Thefe Lawes which were made fucceffively in divers former years, we have reduced under feverall heads in an alphabeticall method, that fo they might the more readilye be found, & that the divers lawes concerning one matter being placed together the fcope and intent of the whole and of every of them might the more eafily be apprehended: we muft confeffe we have not been fo exact in placing every law under its moft proper title as we might, and would have been: the reafon was our hafty indeavour to fatisfie your longing expectation, and frequent complaints for want of fuch a volume to be publifhed in print: wherin (upon every occafion) you might readily fee the rule which you ought to walke by. And in this (we hope) you will finde fatisfaction, by the help of the references under the feverall heads, and the Table which we have added in the end. For fuch lawes and orders as are not of generall concernment we have not put them into this booke, but they remain ftill in force, and are to be feen in the booke of the Records of the Court, but all generall lawes not heer inferted nor mentioned to be ftill of force are to be accounted repealed.

You have called us from amongft the reft of our Bretheren and given us power to make thefe lawes: we muft now call upon you to fee them executed: remembring that old & true proverb, The execution of the law is the life of the law. *If one fort of you viz: non-Freemen fhould object that you had no hand in calling us to this worke, and therfore think yourfelvs not bound to obedience &c. Wee anfwer that a fubfequent, or implicit confent is of like force in this cafe, as an expreffe precedent power: for in putting your perfons and eftates into the protection and way of fubfiftance held forth and exercifed within this Jurifdiction, you doe tacitly fubmit to this Government and to all the wholefome lawes therof, and fo is the common repute in all nations and that upon this* Maxim. Qui fentit commodum fentire debet et onus.

If any of you meet with fome law that feemes not to tend to your particular benefit, you muft confider that lawes are made with refpect to the whole people, and not to each particular perfon: and obedience to them muft be yeilded with refpect to the common welfare, not to thy private advantage, and as thou yeildeft obedience to the law for common good, but to thy difadvantage: fo another muft obferve fome other law for thy good, though to his own damage; thus muft we be content to bear õanothers burden and fo fullfill the Law of Chrift.

That diftinction which is put between the Lawes of God and the lawes of men, becomes a fnare to many as it is mif-applyed in the ordering of their obedience to civil Authoritie; for when the Authoritie is of God and that in way of an Ordinance Rom. 13. 1. *and when the adminiftration of it is according to deductions, and rules gathered from the word of God, and the clear light of nature in civil nations, furely there is no humane law that tendeth to commõ good (according to thofe principles) but the fame is mediately a law of God, and that in way of an Ordinance which all are to fubmit unto and that for confcience fake.* Rom. 13. 5.

By order of the Generall Court.

JNCREASE NOWEL

SECR.

THE
BOOK OF THE GENERAL LAUUES AND LIBERTYES CONCERNING &c:

F*ORASMUCH as the free fruition of fuch Liberties, Immunities, priviledges as humanitie, civilitie & chriftianity call for as due to everie man in his place, & proportion, without impeachmẽt & infringement hath ever been, & ever will be the tranquillity & ftability of Churches & Comon-wealths; & the deniall or deprivall therof the difturbance, if not ruine of both:*

Jt is therfore ordered by this Court, & Authority therof, That no mans life fhall be taken away; no mans honour or good name fhall be ftayned; no mans perfon fhal be arrefted, reftrained, bannifhed, difmembred nor any wayes punifhed; no man fhall be deprived of his wife or children; no mans goods or eftate fhal be taken away from him; nor any wayes indamaged under colour of Law or countenance of Authoritie unles it be by the vertue or equity of fome expreffe law of the Country warranting the fame eftablifhed by a General Court & fufficiently publifhed; or in cafe of the defect of a law in any particular cafe by the word of God. And in capital cafes, or in cafes concerning difmẽbring or banifhmẽt according to that word to be judged by the General Court [1641

Abilitie.

All perfons of the age of twenty one years, and of right underftanding & memorie whether excõmunicate, condemned or other, fhall have full power and libertie to make their Wills & Teftaments & other lawfull Alienations of their lands and eftates. [1641] *fee children.*

> Excõmũicate & condemned perfons may dis pofe of their eftates

Actions.

All Actions of debt, accounts, flaunder, and Actions of the cafe concerning debts and accounts fhal henceforth be tryed where the Plantiffe pleafeth; fo it be in the jurisdiction of that Court where the Plantiffe, or Defendant dwelleth: unles by confent under both their hands it appeare they would have the cafe tryed in any other Court. All other Actions fhal be tryed within that jurisdiction where the caufe of the Action doth arife. [1642]

> where all actiõs fhal be tryed.

2 Jt is ordered by this Court & Authoritie therof, That every perfon impleading another in any court of Affiftants, or County court fhal pay the fum of ten fhillings before his cafe be entred, vnles the court fee caufe to admit any to fue in *forma pauperis.* [1642]

> Fees 10 fs.

3 Jt is ordered by the Authority aforefayd, That where the debt or damage recovered fhall amount to ten pounds in every fuch cafe to pay five fhillings more, and where it fhall amount to twenty pounds or upward there to pay ten fhillings more then the firft ten fhillings, which fayd additions fhall be put to the Iudgement and Execution to be levied by the Marfhall and accounted for to the Treafurer. [1647]

> more 5 fs.
> more 10 fs.

4 In all actions brought to any court the Plantiffe fhall have liberty to withdraw his action or to be non-futed before the Jurie have given in their verdict; in which cafe he fhall alwayes pay full coft and charges to the Defendant, and may afterward renew his fute at another Court. [1641] *fee Caufes. fee Records.*

> Libertie to withdraw or be nonfuted.

Age.

Jt is ordered by this Court & the Authoritie therof, that the age for paffing away of lands, or fuch kinde of hereditaments, or for giving of votes, verdicts or fentences in any civil courts or caufes, fhall be twenty and one years: but in cafe of chufing of Guardions, fourteen years. [1641 1647]

> Full age and Age of difcretion.

Ana-Baptifts.

Forafmuch as experience hath plentifully & often proved that fince the firft arifing of the Ana-baptifts about a hundred years paft they have been the Incendiaries of Common-wealths & the Infectors of perfons in main matters of Religiõ, & the Troublers of Churches in moft places where they have been, & that they who have held the baptizing of Infants ũlawful, have ufually held other errors or herefies together therwith (though as hereticks ufe to doe they have concealed the fame untill they efpied a fit advantage and opportunity to vent them by way of queftion or fcruple) and wheras divers of

A 3   *this*

this kinde have ſince our cõming into New-England appeared amongſt our ſelvs, ſome wherof as others before them have denied the Ordinance of Magiſtracy, and the lawfulnes of making warre, others the lawfulnes of Magiſtrates, and their Inſpection into any breach of the firſt Table: which opinions if cõnived at by us are like to be increaſed among us & ſo neceſſarily bring guilt upõ us, infection, & trouble to the Churches & hazzard to the whole Common-wealth:

Oppoſe Bapt: &c.

Jt is therfore ordered by this Court & Authoritie therof, that if any perſon or perſons within this Iuriſdiction ſhall either openly condemn or oppoſe the baptizing of Infants, or goe about ſecretly to ſeduce others from the approbation or uſe therof, or ſhal purpoſely depart the Congregation at the adminiſtration of that Ordinance; or ſhal deny the Ordinance of Magiſtracy, or their lawfull right or authoritie to make war, or to puniſh the outward breaches of the firſt Table, and ſhall appear to the Court wilfully

continue obſtinate. Baniſhed.

and obſtinately to continue therin, after due meanes of conviction, everie ſuch perſon or perſons ſhall be ſentenced to Baniſhment. [1644]

Appeale.

Jt is ordered by this Court and the Authoritie therof, that it ſhall be in the libertie of every man caſt, condemned, or ſentenced in any Inferiour Court, to make his appeal to the Court of Aſſiſtants. As alſo to appeal from the ſentence of one Magiſtrate, and

Appeal to ſhire Courts.

other perſons deputed to hear and determine ſmall cauſes, unto the ſhire Courts of each Juriſdiction where the cauſe was determined. Provided they tender their appeal and put in ſecuritie before the Iudges of the Court or other perſons authorized to admit Appeals to proſecute it to effect; and alſo to ſatisfie all damages before execution granted,

Securitie to proſecute &c. Execution reſpited. Criminal cauſes

which ſhal not be till twelve hours after judgement, except by ſpecial order of the court: and if the cauſe be of a criminal and not capital nature [in which caſe wee admit no appeal unles where two of five or three of ſix or ſeven, or ſuch a proportion of the number of Magiſtrates or other Iudges then preſent ſhall actually diſſent] then alſo to put in ſecuritie for the good behaviour and appearance at the ſame time. And if the point of appeal

Matter of [[Law
[Fact

be in matter of law then to be determined by the Bench: if in matter of fact, by the Bench and Iurie. And it is further ordered that all appeales with the ſecuritie as aforeſayd ſhall be recorded at the charge of the partie appealing and certified unto the Court to which they are made.

2 Wheras the Countrye is put to great charges by this Court's attending ſutes commenced or renewed either by appeal, petition or review: It is ordered by this Court & Authoritie therof, That in all ſuch caſes if it appear to the Court that the Plantiffe in any ſuch action, appeal, petition or review hath no juſt cauſe of any ſuch proceeding the ſaid Plantiffe ſhall bear the whole charges of the Court both for time and expences which they ſhall judge to have been expended by his occaſion: and may further impoſe a fine upon him as the merit of the cauſe ſhall require, but if they ſhal finde the Defendant in fault they ſhall impoſe the charges upon ſuch Defendant. [1642] [1647] *ſee cauſes. ſee High-wayes. ſee Lying. ſee Townſhips*;

Appearance Non-apearance.

Jt is ordered by this Court and Authoritie therof, That no man ſhall be puniſhed for not appeariug at or before any civil Aſſemblie, Court, Council, Magiſtrate or Officer; nor for the omiſſion of any Office or ſervice if he ſhall be neceſſarily hindred by any apparent act or providence of God which he could neither foreſee nor avoid: provided that this law ſhall not prejudice any perſon of his juſt coſt and damage in any civil Actiõ. [1641] *ſee Armes. ſee Indians. ſee Military. ſee Summons.*

Arreſts.

Jt is ordered and decreed by this Court & Authoritie therof, That no mans perſon

None arreſted or impriſoned.

ſhall be arreſted or impriſoned for any debt or fine if the law can finde any competent meanes of ſatisfaction otherwiſe from his eſtate. And if not his perſon may be arreſted and impriſoned, where he ſhall be kept at his own charge, not the Plantiffs, till ſatisfaction be made; unles the Court that had cognifance of the cauſe or ſome ſuperiour Court ſhall otherwiſe determine: provided nevertheleſſe that no mans perſon ſhall be kept in priſon for debt but when there appears ſome eſtate which he will not

produce

produce, to which end any Court or Commiſſioners authorized by the General Court may adminiſter an oath to the partie or any others ſuſpected to be privie in concealing his eſtate, but ſhall ſatiſfie by ſervice if the Creditor require it but ſhall not be ſolde to any but of the Engliſh nation. [1641: 1647] *ſee ſect* 1. *page* 1.

Attachments.

Jt is ordered by this Court and Authoritie therof that no attachment ſhall be granted in any civil action to any Forreigner againſt a ſetled Inhabitant in this Juriſdiction before he hath given ſufficient ſecuritie or caution to proſecute his action and to anſwer the defendant ſuch coſts as the Court ſhall award him.   And further it is ordered that in all attachments of goods and chattels, or of lands, or hereditaments legall notice ſhall be given unto the partie or left in writing at his houſe, or place of uſuall aboad, otherwiſe the ſute ſhall not proceed; notwithſtanding if he be out of this Juriſdiction the cauſe ſhall then proceed to triall, but judgement ſhall not be entered before the next court.   And if the Defendant doe nor then appear judgement ſhall be entered but execution ſhall not be granted before the Plantiffe hath given ſecuritie to be reſponſall to the Defendant if he ſhall reverſe the judgement within one year or ſuch further time as the Court ſhall limit. [1644] *ſee actions. ſee El. writts. ſee Preſidents. ſee Rates. ſee Recorder.*

(margin: Forreigner ſhal not attach Inhabitãts wᵗout cautiõ.)
(margin: Reſpit of judgment. Of execution.)

Bakers.

Jt is ordered by this Court and Authoritie therof, that henceforth every Baker ſhall have a diſtinct mark for his bread, & keep the true aſſizes as heerafter is expreſſed *viz.* When wheat is ordinarily ſold at theſe ſeverall rates heerafter mentioned the peñie white loaf by averdupois weight ſhall weigh when wheat is by the buſhell - - - - - - - -

at	fs.	d.	The white oũces	qr.	wheaten oũc.	qr.	houfhould oũc.	
at 3	fs.	o d.	11	1	17	1	23	o.
at 3		6	10	1	15	1	20	2.
at 4		o	09	1	14	o	18	2.
at 4		6	08	1	11	3	16	2.
at 5		o	07	3	11	2	15	2.
at 5		6	07	o	10	2	14	o.
at 6		o	06	2	10	o	13	o.
at 6		6	06	o	09	2	12	2.

and ſo proportionably: under the penaltie of forfeiting all ſuch bread as ſhall not be of the ſeverall aſſizes as is aforementioned to the uſe of the poor of the towne where the offence is committed, and otherwiſe as is heerafter expreſſed: and for the better execution of this preſent Order ; there ſhall be in everie market towne, and all other townes needfull, one or two able perſons annually choſen by each towne, who ſhall be ſworn at the next county Court. or by the next Magiſtrate, unto the faithfull diſcharge of his or their office; who are heerby authorized to enter into all houſes, either with a Conſtable or without where they ſhall ſuſpect or be informed of any bread baked for ſale: & alſo to weigh the ſaid bread as oft as they ſee cauſe: and to ſeize all ſuch as they finde defective.   As alſo to weigh all butter made up for ſale; and bringing unto, or being in the towne or market to be ſolde by weight: which if found light after notice once given ſhall be forfeited in like manner.   The like penaltie ſhall be for not marking all bread made for ſale.   and the ſayd officer ſhall have one third part of all forfeitures for his paines; the reſt to the poor as aforeſayd. [1646]

(margin: Penaltie.)
(margin: Clerk of market. Their power.)
(margin: Butter.)
(margin: bread not marked. Clerks fee.)

Ballaſt.

Jt is ordered by this Court and Authoritie therof; that no ballaſt ſhall be taken frõ any towne ſhore by any perſon whatſoever without allowance under the hands of the ſelect men upon the penalty of ſixpence for every ſhovel-full ſo taken; unles ſuch ſtones as they had layd there hefore.   2 Jt is alſo ordered by the Authoritie aforeſayd; that no ſhip nor other veſſell ſhall caſt out any ballaſt in the chanel, or other place inconvenient, in any Harbour within this Juriſdiction upon the penaltie of ten pounds. [1646-1642]

(margin: Penaltie.)
(margin: Penaltie.)

Barratrie.

Jt is ordered, decreed and by this Court declared; that if any man be proved
and

and judged a common barrater, vexing others with unjuſt, frequent and endles ſutes: it
ſhall be in the power of Courts both to rejeⱦ his cauſe and to puniſh him for his Bar-
ratrie. [1641]

Benevolence.

Jt is decreed, that this Court heerafter will graunt no benevolence, except in for-
reigne occaſions & when there is mony in the Treaſurie ſufficient and our debts firſt ſa-
tiſfied. [1641]

Bills.

Jt is ordered by the Authority of this Court that any debt, or debts due upon bill,
or other ſpecialtie aſſigned to another; ſhall be as good a debt & eſtate to the Aſſignee
as it was to the Aſſigner at the time of it's aſſignation.   And that it ſhall be lawfull for
the ſayd Aſſignee to ſue for and recover the ſaid debt, due upon bill, and ſo aſſigned, as
fully as the originall creditor might have done, provided the ſaid aſſignement be made
upon the backſide of the bill or ſpecialtie. [1647] *ſee uſurie.*

Bond-ſlavery.

Jt is ordered by this Court and authoritie therof, that there ſhall never be any
bond-ſlavery, villenage or captivitie amongſt us; unleſſe it be lawfull captives, taken in
juſt warrs, and ſuch ſtrangers as willingly ſell themſelves, or are ſolde to us: and ſuch
ſhall have the libertyes and chriſtian uſages which the law of God eſtabliſhed in Iſraell
concerning ſuch perſons doth morally require, provided, this exempts none from ſervi-
tude who ſhall be judged thereto by Authoritie. [1641]

Bounds of townes and perſons.

Foraſmuch as the bounds of townes & of the lands of particular perſons are carefully to be maintained, & not without great danger to be removed by any, which notwithſtanding by deficiency and decay of marks, may at unawars be done,   whereby
great jealouſies of perſons, trouble in townes and incumbrances in courts do often ariſe,
which by due care and meanes might be prevented: - - -

Boundes of
towne ſet out
within 12 mon.

Perambulation

Jt is therefore ordered by this Court and the Authoritie therof, that every towne
ſhall ſet out their bounds within twelve months after their bounds are graunted. And
that when their bounds are once ſet out: once in the year three or more perſons of a
towne, appoynted by the ſeleⱦ men, ſhall appoynt with the adjacent townes to go the
bounds betwixt their ſaid townes, and renew their marks; which marks ſhal be a great
heap of ſtones, or a trench of ſix foot long and two foot broad. The moſt ancient town
to give notice of the time and place of meeting for this perambulation.   Which time

Jn 1 or 2 mõ.
on payn of 5 li

ſhall be in the firſt or ſecond month, upon payne of five pounds for everie towne that
ſhall negleⱦ the ſame; provided that the three men appoynted for perambulation ſhall
goe in their ſeverall quarters by order of the Seleⱦ men and at the charge of the ſeverall
townes.

Particular per
ambu:

Pænalty 10 ſs.

And it is further ordered that if any particular proprietor of lands lying in common with others ſhall refuſe to goe the bounds betwixt his land and other mens once a
yeare in the firſt or ſecond month, being requeſted therunto upon one weeks warning,
he ſhall forfeit for every day ſoe negleⱦing, ten ſhillings, halfe to the partie moving
thereto, the other halfe to the towne. [1641 1647]

Burglarie and Theft.

Foraſmuch as many perſons of late years have been, and are apt to be injurious to
the goods and lives of others, notwithſtanding all care and meanes to prevent and puniſh the ſame; - - -

Houſe, field or
high wayes.
Firſt offence.

Third offence
death.

Jt is therefore ordered by this Court and Authoritie therof that if any perſon ſhall
commit Burglarie by breaking up any dwelling houſe, or ſhall rob any perſon in the
field, or high wayes; ſuch a perſon ſo offending ſhall for the firſt offence be branded
on the forehead with the letter (𝓑) If he ſhall offend in the ſame kinde the ſecond
time, he ſhall be branded as before and alſo be ſeverally whipped: and if he ſhall fall
into the like offence the third time he ſhall be put to death, as being incorrigible. And
if any perſon ſhal commit ſuch Burglarie, or rob in the fields or houſe on the Lords day
besides

besides the former punishments, he shal for the first offence have one of his ears cut off. And for the second offence in the same kinde he shal loose his other ear in the same mã-ner. And if he fall into the same offence a third time he shal be put to death if it appear to the Court he did it presumptuously. [1642 1647]

Lords day.

2 For the prevention of Pilfring and Theft, it is ordered by this Court and Authori-tie therof; that if any person shal be taken or known to rob any orchard or garden, that shall hurt, or steal away any grafts or fruit trees, fruits, linnen, woollen, or any other goods left out in orchards, gardens, backsides, or any other place in house or fields: or shall steal any wood or other goods from the water-side, from mens doors, or yards; he shall forfeit treble damage to the owners therof. And if they be children, or servants that shall trespasse heerin, if their parents or masters will not pay the penaltie before ex-pressed, they shal be openly whipped. And forasmuch as many times it so falls out that small thefts and other offences of a criminall nature, are committed both by English & Indian, in townes remote from any prison, or other fit place to which such malefactors may be committed till the next Court, it is therfore heerby ordered; that any Magistrate upon complaint made to him may hear, and upon due proof determin any such small of-fences of the aforesayd nature, according to the laws heer established, and give warrant to the Constable of that town where the offender lives to levie the same: provided the damage or fine exceed not fourty shillings: provided also it shall be lawfull for either partie to appeal to the next Court to be holden in that Jurisdiction, giving sufficient caution to prosecute the same to effect at the said Court. And everie Magistrate shall make return yearly to the Court of that Jurisdiction wherin he liveth of what cases he hath so ended. And also the Constables of all such fines as they have received. And where the offender hath nothing to satisfie such Magistrate may punish by stocks, or whipping as the cause shall deserve, not exceeding ten stripes. It is also ordered that all servants & workmen imbeazling the goods of their masters, or such as set them on work shal make restitution and be lyable to all lawes & penalties as other men. [1646]

Rob [orchard. [garden. Steal goods.

Treble damage.

Whipped.

One Magistr: may hear & de-termine.

Appeal. Magistrate and Côst: to make return

stocks or whip

Servants and workmen.

CAPITAL LAWES.

I F any man after legal conviction shall HAVE OR WORSHIP any other God, but the LORD GOD: he shall be put to death. *Exod.* 22. 20. *Deut.* 13. 6. & 10. *Deut.* 17. 2. 6.

Idolatrie.

2 If any man or woman be a WITCH, that is, hath or consulteth with a familiar spirit, they shall be put to death. *Exod.* 22. 18. *Levit.* 20. 27. *Deut.* 18. 10. 11.

Witch-craft.

3 If any person within this Jurisdiction whether Christian or Pagan shall wittingly and willingly presume to BLASPHEME the holy Name of God, Father, Son or Holy-Ghost, with direct, expresse, presumptuous, or high-handed blasphemy, either by wilfull or obstinate denying the true God, or his Creation, or Government of the world: or shall curse God in like manner, or reproach the holy Religion of God as if it were but a politick device to keep ignorant men in awe; or shal utter any other kinde of Blasphemy of the like nature & degree they shall be put to death. *Levit.* 24. 15. 16.

Blasphemie.

4 If any person shall commit any wilfull MURTHER, which is Man slaughter, committed upon premeditate malice, hatred, or crueltie not in a mans necessary and just defence, nor by meer casualty against his will, he shall be put to death. *Exod.* 21. 12. 13. *Numb.* 35. 31.

Murther.

5 If any person slayeth another suddenly in his ANGER, or CRUELTY of passion, he shall be put to death. *Levit.* 24. 17. *Numb.* 35. 20. 21.

6 If any person shall slay another through guile, either by POYSONING, or o-ther such devilish practice, he shall be put to death. *Exod.* 21. 14.

Poysoning.

7 If any man or woman shall LYE WITH ANY BEAST, or bruit creature, by car-nall copulation; they shall surely be put to death: and the beast shall be slain, & buri-ed, and not eaten. *Lev.* 20. 15. 16.

Bestialitie.

8 If any man LYETH WITH MAN-KINDE as he lieth with a woman, both of them have committed abomination, they both shal surely be put to death: unles the one partie were forced (or be under fourteen years of age in which case he shall be seveerly

Sodomie. Genis. 19. 5.

B   punished punifhed) *Levit.* 20. 13.

Adulterie.

9 If any perfon commit ADULTERIE with a married, or efpoufed wife; the Adulterer & Adultereffe fhal furely be put to death. *Leb.* 20. 19. & 18. 20. *Deu.* 22. 23. 27

Man-ftealing.

10 If any man STEALETH A MAN, or Man-kinde, he fhall furely be put to death *Exodus* 21. 16.

Falfe-wittnes.

11 If any man rife up by FALSE-WITNES wittingly, and of purpofe to take away any mans life: he fhal be put to death. *Deut.* 19. 16. 18. 16.

Confpiracie.

12 If any man fhall CONSPIRE, and attempt any Invafion, Infurrection, or publick Rebellion againft our Common-Wealth: or fhall indeavour to furprize any Town, or Townes, Fort, or Forts therin; or fhall treacheroufly, & perfidioufly attempt the Alteration and Subverfion of our frame of Politie, or Government fundamentally he fhall be put to death. *Numb.* 16. 2 *Sam.* 3. 2 *Sam.* 18. 2 *Sam.* 20.

Child curfe or fmite parẽts

13 If any child, or children, above fixteen years old, and of fufficient underftanding, fhall CURSE, or SMITE their natural FATHER, or MOTHER; he or they fhall be put to death: unles it can be fufficiently teftified that the Parents have been very unchriftianly negligent in the education of fuch children; or fo provoked them by extream, and cruel correction; that they have been forced therunto to preferve themfelves from death or maiming. *Exod.* 21. 17. *Lev.* 20. 9. *Exod.* 21. 15.

Rebellious Sõ

14 If a man have a ftubborn or REBELLIOUS SON, of fufficient years & ŭderftanding (*viz*) fixteen years of age, which will not obey the voice of his Father, or the voice of his Mother, and that when they have chaftened him will not harken unto them: then fhal his Father & Mother being his natural parẽts, lay hold on him, & bring him to the Magiftrates affembled in Court & teftifie unto them, that their Son is ftubborn & rebellious & will not obey their voice and chaftifement, but lives in fundry notorious crimes, fuch a fon fhal be put to death. *Deut.* 21. 20. 21.

Rape.

15 If any man fhal RAVISH any maid or fingle womã, cõmitting carnal copulation with her by force, againft her own will; that is above the age of ten years he fhal be punifhed either with death, or with fome other greivous punifhmẽt according to circumftances as the Judges, or General court fhal determin. [1641]

Cask & Cooper.

London affize.

Gager

his Fee.

Who fhall appoint Gager.

Coopers brand

It is ordered by this Court and authoritie therof, that all cask ufed for any liquor, fifh, or other cõmoditie to be put to fale fhall be of London affize , and that fit perfons fhal be appointed from time to time in all places needfull, to gage all fuch veffels or cask & fuch as fhal be found of due affize fhal be marked with the Gagers mark, & no other who fhal have for his paines four pence for every tun, & fo proportionably. And every County court or any one Magiftrate upon notice given them fhall appoint fuch Gagers to view the faid cask, & to fee that they be right, & of found & wel feafoned timber, & that everie Cooper have a diftinct brand-mark on his own cask, upon payn of forfeiture of twenty fhilling in either cafe, & fo proportiõably for leffer veffels. [1642 1647]

Cattel. Corn-fields. Fences.

each party make good his fence.
No catle put in till corn be out

It is ordered by this Court and authoritie therof, That in all corn-fields, which are inclofed in common: everie partie interefted therin, fhall from time to time make good his part of the fence, and fhall not put in any cattel, fo long as any corn fhal be upon any part of it, upon payn to anfwer all the damage which fhal come therby. [1647]

Occupiers of land may order cõmon fields

2 *Wheras it is foũd by experience that there hath been much trouble & difference in feverall toẁnes, about the fencing, planting, foẁing, feeding & ordering of common fields,* It is therfore ordered by this Court & authoritie therof, that where the occupiers of the land, or of the greateft part therof cãnot agree about the fencing or improvmẽt of fuch their faid fields, that thẽ the Select men in the feveral towns fhal order the fame, or in cafe where no fuch are, then the major part of the Freemen (with what convenient fpeed they may) fhal determin any fuch difference, as may arife upon any informatiõ given them by the faid occupiers, excepting fuch occupier's land as fhal be fufficiently fenced in by it felfe, which

Exc: pertic: fenced.

any occupier of land may lawfully doe. [1643. 1647]

3 *Wheras this Court hath long fince probided that all men fhall fence their corn, meadoẁ*
ground

ground and fuch like againft great cattle, to the end the increafe of cattle efpecially of cowes and their breed fhould not be hindred, there being then but few horfes in the countrie, which fince are much increafed, many wherof run in a fort wilde, doing much damage in corn and other things, notwithftanding fences made up according to the true intent of the order in that cafe eftablifhed: many wherof are unknown, moft fo unruly that they can by no means be caught, or got into cuftodie, wherby their owners might anfwer damages: & if fometimes with much difficultie and charge they be; they are in danger of perifhing before the owner appears or can be found out: all which to prevent,

It is ordered by this Court & authoritie therof; That everie towne and peculiar in this Jurisdictiõ, fhall henceforth give fome diftinct Brand-mark appointed by this court (a coppie of which marks each Clerk of writs in everie town fhal keep a record of) upon the horn, or left buttock or fhoulder of all their cattle which feed in open cõmon without conftant keepers, wherby it may be known to what town they doe belong. And if any trefpaffe not fo marked they fhall pay double damages: nor fhall any perfon know- | Double damage.
ing, or after due notice given of any beaft of his to be unruly in refpect of fences, fuffer him or them to go in cõmon or againft corn fields, or other impropriate inclofed groũds fenced as aforefaid, without fuch fhackles or fetters as may reftrein and prevent trefpaffe | Fetters.
therin by them from time to time. And if any horfe or other beaft trefpaffe in corn, or other inclofure being fenced in fuch fort as fecures againft cows, oxen and fuch like or- derly cattel: the partie or parties trefpaffed fhall procure two fufficient Inhabitants of that town, of good repute and credit to view and adjudge the harms, which the owner | Harms viewed
of the beaft fhal fatisfie, when known, upõ reafonable demand, whether the beaft were impounded or not. But if the owner be known, or neer refiding as in the fame town or the like, he fhall forthwith have notice of the trefpaffe and damage charged upon him, | Notice of damage.
that if he approve not therof he may nominate one fuch man, who with one fuch other chofen by the partie damnified as aforefaid, fhal review & adjudge the faid harms, pro- vided they agree of damage within one day after due notice given, & that no after harms intervene to hinder it. Which being forthwith difcharged, together with the charge of the notice, former view and determination of damages, the firft judgement fhall be void, or elfe to ftand good in law. And if any cattle be found damage faifant, the par- | Damage faifant
tie damnified may impound or keep them in his own private clofe, or yard till he may give notice to the owner, and if they cannot agree, the owner may replevie them, or the other partie may retur̃ them to the owner & take his remedie according to law. [1647]

4 It is ordered by the authoritie of this Court that for all harms done by goats, there | Goats fhall pay double damage
fhall be double damages allowed: and that any goats taken in corn or gardens, the ow- ners of fuch corn or gardens may keep or ufe the faid goats till full fatisfaction be made by the owners of fuch goats. [1646]

5 *Forafmuch as complaints have been made of a verie evil practice, of fome difordered perfons in the countrie, who ufe to take other mens horfes, fomtimes upon the commons and fomtimes out of their own grounds, and inclofures, and ride them at their pleafure without any leave or privitie of the owners:*

It is therfore ordered and enacted by the authoritie of this Court, that whofoever | Unruly taken
fhall take any other mans horfe, mare, affe or drawing beaft, either out of his inclofure, or upon any common or elfewhere, (except fuch be taken damage faifant and difpofed of according to law) without leave of the owner: & fhall ride or ufe the fame, he fhal pay | Penaltie.
to the partie wronged, treble damages, or if the complainant fhall defire it then to pay only ten fhillings, and fuch as have not to make fatisfaction, fhall be punifhed by whip- | Corporal punifhment
ping, imprifonment, or otherwife as by law fhal be adjudged, and any one Magiftrate or | One Magiftr: power.
County court may hear & determin the fame. [1647]

6 *For the better preferving of corn from damage by all kinde of cattle, and that all fen- ces of corn fields may from time to time be fufficiently upheld and maintained;*

It is therfore ordered that the Select men of every town within this Jurisdiction | Select men to appoint men to view fenc:
fhall appoynt from year to year two (or more if need require) of the Inhabitants therof to view the cõmon fences of everie their corn fields, to the end, to take due notice of the

give notice of defects. Owners to mend in 6 days elfe Viewers to have doubl pay	reall defects and infufficiencie therof, who fhall forthwith acquaint the owners therof with the fame: and if the faid owners do not within fix dayes time or otherwife as the Select men fhall appoint, fufficiently repair their faid defective fences, then the faid two or more Inhabitants appointed as aforefayd fhall forthwith repair or renew them and fhall have double recompence, for all their labour, care, coft and trouble, to be payd by the owners of the faid infufficient fence or fences, and fhall have warrant from the fayd Select men directed to the Conftable to levie the fame, either upon the corn or other e-
upõ due proof	ftate of the delinquent. Provided the defect of the fence or fences be fufficiently proved by two or three wittneffes. [1647]
Partitiõ fenc.	7 Where lands lye in common unfenced, if one man fhall improve his lands by fenc- ing in feverall & another fhall not, he who fhall fo improve fhall fecure his land againft other mens cattle; & fhall not compel fuch as joyne upon him to make any fence with him; except he fhall alfo improve in feverall as the other doth. And where one man fhal improve before his neighbour & fo make the whole fence, if after his faid neighbour fhall improve alfo, he fhal then fatisfie for halfe the others fence againft him, according to the prefent value and fhall maintain the fame: and if the firft man fhall after lay open his faid field, then the fayd neighbour fhal injoye his faid halfe fence fo purchafed to his own ufe, & fhal alfo have libertie to buy the other halfe fence paying according to pre- fent valuation to be fet by two men chofen by either partie one: the like order fhal be where any man fhall improve land againft any town cõmon. provided this order fhall
Houfe lots not exc: 10 acrs.	not extend to houfe lots not exceeding ten acres, but if in fuch, one fhall improve, his neighbour fhal be compellable to make & maintain one half of the fence between them
Infuffi; fence not dam: exc: by fwine, calvs unruly cattle, or wilful fpoil	whether he improve or not. Provided alfo that no man fhall be lyable to fatisfie for da- mage done in any ground not fufficiently fenced except it fhall be for damage done by fwine or calves under a year old, or unruly cattle which will not be reftreined by ordina- ry fences, or where any man fhall put his cattle, or otherwife voluntarily trefpaffe upon his neighbours ground, & if the partie damnified finde the cattle damage faifant he may impound or otherwife difpofe of them as in *Sect:* 3. [1642]

Caufes. Small caufes.

	For eafing the charge & incumbrance of courts by fmall caufes, It is ordered by this Court and authoritie therof, That any Magiftrate in the town where he dwells may
One Magiftr: may end cau: . not exc: 40 fs	hear and determin by his difcretion (not by Jurie) according to the laws heer eftablifhed, all caufes arifing in that County wherin the debt, trefpaffe or damage doth not exceed fourty fhillings, who may fend for parties, & wittneffes by Sũmons or Attachment di- rected to the Conftable who fhall faithfully execute the fame. And it is further ordered
or 3 Cõmiffi:	that in fuch towns where no Magiftrate dwells, the Court of Affiftants or County court for each Shire fhall from time to time upon requeft of the faid towns fignified under the hands of the Conftable appoint three of the Freemen as Commiffioners in fuch cafes any two wherof fhall have like power to hear and determin by their difcretion (not by Jurie)
fend for partys & witneffes. give oath to witneffes.	all fuch caufes aforefaid according to the laws heer eftablifhed, who alfo have heerby power to fend for parties and wittneffes by Sũmons or Attachment directed to the Con- ftable, as alfo to adminifter oaths to wittneffes & to give time to the Defendãt to anfwer if they fee caufe, & if the partie fentenced refufe to give his own bond for appearance or
Cõmif: may charg Conft: with party in fome cafes.	fatisfaction where no goods appear in the fame town where the Plantiffe or Defendant dwells, they may charge the Conftable with the partie to carry him before a Magiftrate or Shire court (if then fitting) to be further proceeded with according to law; but the
fued in any town at Pl: lib	faid three men may not commit to prifon in any cafe. And it is further ordered that fuch as be found in any town fhall be lyable to be fued in that town at libertie of the Plantiff.
	And for afmuch as the Governour, Deputy Governour and Affiftants are under an oath of God for difpencing equal juftice according to law, It is ordered by the Authoritie afore-
Afoc: & Com mif: fworn.	faid; that henceforth all Affociates for County courts when and where there be any; and all fuch Freemẽ authorized as aforefayd, fhall be fworn before each Shire court, or fome Magiftrate in that County unto the faithfull difcharge of the truft and power committed
	to them

to them. And it is further ordered by the Authoritie aforefaid, that in all fmall caufes as aforefayd, where only one Magiftrate dwells within the town, and the caufe concerns himfelfe, as alfo in fuch towns where no Magiftrate is, and the caufe concerns any of the three Freemen aformentioned, that in fuch cafes the five, feven, or other number of Selected townfmen fhall have power to hear and determin the fame: and alfo to graunt execution for the levying, and gathering up fuch damages, for the ufe of the perfon damnified. And any Court may reject any fuch caufe in all the cafes beforementioned in this law, if it were not firft brought to the power heerby authorized in towns to end the fame. [1647]

Charges publick.

Is is ordered by this Court that no Governour, Deputy Govẽ: Affiftant, Affociate, Grand, or Petty Jurie-man, at any court; nor any Deputie for the General court, nor any Cõmiffioner for martial difciplin at the time of their publick meetings; fhall at any time bear his own charges: but their neceffary expences fhal be defrayed either by the town, or the Shire on whofe fervice they are, or by the Country in generall. [1634. 1641]

2 It is ordered by this Court that in all ordinary publick works of the Cõmon-weal, one Affiftant and the Overfeer of the work fhal have power to fend their warrants to the Conftables of the next towns to fend fo many labourers & artificers as the warrant fhall direct, which the Conftable and two other or more of the Freemen which he fhall take to himfelfe fhall forthwith execute: for which fervice fuch Affiftant and Overfeer aforfaid fhall have power to give fuch extraordinary wages as they fhall judge the work to deferve. Provided that for any ordinary work no man fhal be compelled to work from home above a week together. And for all extraordinarie publick works it is ordered that one Affiftant & the Overfeer of the faid work fhall have power to fend their warrants to the Conftable of any town for fo many men of any conditiõ except Magiftrates & Officers of Churches and Cõmon-wealth, as the warrant fhall direct, which the Conftable & two or more that he fhal chufe fhal forthwith fend: to advife & attẽd the fame. 1634

3 *This Court taking into confideration the neceffity of an equal contribution to all common charges in towns, and obferving that the cheif occafion of the defect heerin arifeth from hence, that many of thofe who are not Freemen, nor members of any Church doe take advantage therby to withdraw their help in fuch voluntary contributions as are in ufe.*

It is therfor ordered by this Court and Authoritie therof, That everie Inhabitant fhal henceforth contribute to all charges both in Church & Commonwealth wherof he doth or may receive benefit: and every fuch Inhabitant who fhal not voluntarily contribute proportionably to his ability with the Freemen of the fame town to all comon charges both civil and ecclefiaftical fhall be compelled thereto by affeffment & diftreffe to be levied by the Conftable or other Officer of the town as in other cafes: and that the lands & eftates of all men (wherever they dwell) fhall be rated for all town charges both civil and ecclefiafticall as aforefaid where the lands and eftates fhal lye: their perfons where they dwell. [1638 1643 1644]

4 *For a more equall and ready way of rayfing meanes for defraying publick charges in time to come: and for preventing fuch inconveniences as have fallen out upon former affeffments; It is ordered and enacted by the authoritie of this Court,* That the Treafurer for the time being fhal from year to year in the firft month without expecting any other order fend forth his warrants to the Conftables & Select men of every town within this Jurisdiction, requiring the Conftable to call together the Inhabitants of the town who being fo affembled: fhal chufe fome one of their Freemen to be a Commiffioner for the town, who together with the Select men for their prudential affairs fhall fome time or times in the fixt month then next enfuing make a Lift of all the male perfons in the fame town, from fixteen years old & upwards; and a true eftimation of all perfonall & real eftates, being, or reputed to be the eftate of all & everie the perfons in the fame town, or otherwife under their cuftody, or managing according to juft valuation, and to what perfons the fame doe belong whether in their own town or other where, fo neer as they can by all lawful wayes and means which they may ufe. *viz:* of houfes, lands

B 3   of all

of all forts as well unbroken up as other (except fuch as doth or fhal lye common for free feed of cattle to the ufe of the inhabitants in generall whether belonging to towns, or particular perfons but not to be kept or hearded upõ it to the damage of the Proprietors) mills, fhips & all fmall veffells, merchantable goods, cranes, wharfes & all forts of cattle & all other known eftate whatfoever; as alfo all vifible eftate either at fea or on fhore all which perfons and eftates are by the faid Commiffioners & Selеct men to be affeffed, and rated as heer followeth *viz:* every perfon aforefaid except Magiftrates and Elders of Churches, two fhillings fixpence by the head, & all eftates both reall & perfonall at one pennie for everie twenty fhillings, according to the rates of cattle heerafter mentioned. And for a more certein rule in rating of cattle: everie cow of four year olde and upward fhall be valued at five pounds, everie heifer, and fteer betwixt three and four years old four pounds, and between two & three years old at fifty fhillings, and between one and two years thirty fhillings: everie ox & bull of four year old & upward fix pounds. Everie horfe & mare of four year old and upward feven pounds, of three year old five poũds between two and three year old three pounds, of one year old fourtie fhillings. Everie fheep above one year old thirty fhillings: everie goat above one year old eight fhillings: everie fwine above one year old twenty fhillings: everie affe above one year old fourty fhillings. And all cattel of all forts under a year old are heerby exempted, as alfo all hay and corn in the husbandmans hand, becaufe all meadow, arrable ground and cattle are ratable as aforefaid. And for all fuch perfons as by the advantage of their arts & trades are more enabled to help bear the publick charge then common laborours and workmẽ, as Butchers, Bakers, Brewers, Victuailers, Smiths, Carpenters, Taylors, fhoe-makers, Joyners, Barbers, Millers & Mafons with all other manuall perfons & artifts, fuch are to be rated for their returns & gains proportionable unto other men for the produce of their eftates. Provided that in the rate by the poll, fuch perfons as are difabled by ficknes, lamenes or other infirmitie fhall be exempted. And for fuch fervants & children as take not wages, their parents and mafters fhall pay for them, but fuch as take wages fhal pay for themfelves. And it is further ordered that the Cõmiffioners for the feverall towns in everie Shire fhall yearly upon the firft fourth day of the week in the feventh month, affemble at their fhire Town: & bring with them fairly written the juft number of males lifted as aforefaid, and the affeffments of eftates made in their feveral towns according to the rules & directions in this prefent order expreffed, and the faid Cõmiffioners being fo affembled fhall duly and carefully examin all the faid lifts and affeffments of the feverall towns in that Shire, and fhall correct & perfect the fame according to the true intent of this order, as they or the major part of them fhal determĩ, & the fame fo perfected they fhal fpeedily tranfmit to the Treafurer ũder their hands or the hands of the major part of them and therupon the Treafurer fhal give warrants to the Conftables to collect & levie the fame; fo as the whole affeffment both for perfons & eftates may be payd in unto the Treafurer before the twentith day of the ninth mõth, yearly, & everie one fhal pay their rate to the Conftable in the fame town where it fhal be affeffed. Nor fhall any land or eftate be rated in any other town but where the fame fhal lye, is, or was improved to the owners, reputed owners or other propietors ufe or behoof if it be within this Jurisdictiõ. And if the Treafurer cañot difpofe of it there, the Conftable fhal fend it to fuch place in *Boſton* or elfwhere as the Treafurer fhall appoint at the charge of the Countrie to be allowed the Conftable upon his accoũt with the Treafurer. And for all peculiars *viz:* fuch places as are not yet layd within the bounds of any town the fame lands with the perfons and eftates therupon fhall be affeffed by the rates of the town next unto it, the meafure or eftimation fhall be by the diftance of the Meeting houfes.

And if any of the faid Commiffioners or of the Select men fhall wittingly fail or neglect to perform the truft committed to them by this Order in not making, correcting, perfecting or tranfmitting any of the faid Lifts or Affeffments according to the intent of this Order; everie fuch offendor fhall be fined fourty fhillings for everie fuch offence, or fo much as the Country fhall be damnified therby, fo as it exceed not fourty fhillings for one offence. Provided that fuch offence or offences be
complained

All known & vifible eftate

Perfons exempt: frõ pol mony 1 *d.* in the *li.* upon eftate.

Rates of cattle

Artificers &c

Impotent perfons exempt: frõ pol mony

Cõmiffi: meet in 7 month at Shire town

to perfect affeffments.

Conftable to collect & pay in 9 mõth.

Land rated where it lyes

Peculiars

Commiffi: or Select men defaulting

fined 40 fs.

complained of and profecuted in due courfe of law within fix months. And it is farther ordered that upon all diftreffes to be taken for any of the rates and affeffments aforefaid: the Officer fhall diftrein goods, or cattle if they may be had, and if no goods then lands or houfes, if neither goods nor lands can be had within the town where fuch diftreffe is to be taken, then upon fuch return to the Treafurer he fhall give warrant to attach the body of fuch perfon to be carried to prifon, there to be kept till the next court of that Shire; except they put in fecuritie for their appearance there, or that payment be made in the mean time . And it is farther ordered that the prizes of all forts of corn to be re-ceived upon any rate, by vertue of this order, fhall be fuch as this Court fhall fet from year to year; and in default therof they fhall be accepted at the prcie current to be judg-ed by the fayd Commiffioners of Effex, Midlefex and Suffolk. And it is farther order-ed that all eftates of land in England fhall not be rated in any publick affeffment. And it is heerby declared that by publick rates and affeffments , is intended only fuch as are affeffed by order of the General court for the coñtrys occafion & no other. [1646 1647]
if profecuted fix mon. Conft: direct:
Prizes of corn
Lands in Eng-land exempt: Intent of pub-lick rates.

Children.

Forafmuch as the good education of children is of fingular behoof and benefit to any Com-mon-wealth; and wher as many parents & mafters are too indulgent and negligent of their duty in that kinde. It is therfore ordered that the Select men of everie town, in the feverall precincts and quarters where they dwell, fhall have a vigilant eye over their brethren & neighbours, to fee, firft that none of them fhall fuffer fo much barbarifm in any of their families as not to indeavour to teach by themfelves or others, their children & apprenti-ces fo much learning as may inable them perfectly to read the englifh tongue, & know-ledge of the Capital lawes: upõ penaltie of twentie fhillings for each neglect therin. Alfo that all mafters of families doe once a week (at the leaft) catechize their children and fer-vants in the grounds & principles of Religion, & if any be unable to doe fo much: that then at the leaft they procure fuch children or apprentices to learn fome fhort orthodox catechifm without book, that they may be able to anfwer unto the queftions that fhall be propounded to them out of fuch catechifm by their parents or mafters or any of the Select men when they fhall call them to a tryall of what they have learned in this kinde. And further that all parents and mafters do breed & bring up their children & apprenti-ces in fome honeft lawful calling, labour or imploymẽt, either in husbandry, or fome o-ther trade profitable for themfelves, and the Common-wealth if they will not or cannot train them up in learning to fit them for higher imployments. And if any of the Select men after admonitiõ by them given to fuch mafters of families fhal finde them ftill neg-ligent of their dutie in the particulars aforementioned, wherby children and fervants be-come rude, ftubborn & unruly; the faid Select men with the help of two Magiftrates, or the next County court for that Shire, fhall take fuch children or apprentices from them & place them with fome mafters for years (boyes till they come to twenty one, and girls eighteen years of age compleat) which will more ftrictly look unto, and force them to fubmit unto government according to the rules of this order, if by fair means and former inftructions they will not be drawn unto it. [1642]
Care of Se-lect men
ᵗ y all children may read on pen: of 20 fs.
Catechifm.
Unruly child-ren
placed forth

2 *Wheras fundry Gentlemen of qualitie, and others oft times fend over their children into this country unto fome freinds heer, hoping at the leaft therby to prevent their extravagant and riotous courfes, who notwithftanding by means of fome unadvifed and ill-affected perfons, which give them credit, in expectation their freinds, either in favour to them, or prevention of blemifh to themfelves, will difcharge what ever is done that way, they are no leffe lavifh & profufe heer to the great greif of their freinds, difhonour of God & reproach of the Countrie.*
Extravagancy

It is therfore ordered by this Court & authoritie therof; That if any perfon after publication heerof fhall any way give credit to any fuch youth, or other perfon under twentie one years of age, without order from fuch their freinds, heer, or elfwhere, under their hands in writing they fhall lofe their debt whatever it be . And further if fuch youth or other perfon incur any penalty by fuch means and have not wherwith to pay, fuch perfon, or perfons, as are occafions therof fhall pay it as delinquents in the like cafe fhould doe. [1647] *See Abilitie.*
Debts of per fons in nõage not recov.
occafiõers of their difor: to pay their fine.

3 If any

Parents denying marriage

3 If any parents fhall wilfully, and unreafonably deny any childe timely or conveni-ent marriage, or fhall exercife any unnaturall feveritie towards them, fuch children fhal have libertie to complain to Authoritie for redreffe in fuch cafes. [1641]

Orphan not difpofed of but by confent of Authority.

Minority of women.

4 No Orphan during their minority which was not committed to tuition, or fervice by their parents in their life time, fhall afterward be abfolutely difpofed of by any with-out the confent of fome Court wherin two Affiftants (at leaft) fhall be prefent, except in cafe of marriage, in which the approbation of the major part of the Select men, in that town or any one of the next Affiftants fhall be fufficient. And the minoritie of women in cafe of marriage fhall be till fixteen years. [1646] *See Age. Cap: Laws. Lib: cōmō: marriage.*

Clerk of writs.

It is ordered by this Court and Authoritie therof ; that in everie town throughout this Jurifdiction there fhall henceforth be a Clerk of the writs nominated by each town and allowed by each fhire Court, or court of Affiftants to graunt Summons and Attach-ments in all civil actions : and attachments (or Summons at the libertie of the Plantiffe) fhall be graunted when the partie is a ftranger not dwelling amongft us or for fome that are going out of our Jurifdiction, or that are about to make away their eftates to defraud

Doubtful in e-ftate.

their creditors, or when perfons are doubtfull in their eftates not only to the Plantiffe, but to the Clerk of the writs, fignified ūder the hands of two honeft perfons, neer dwel-

Cl: grant repl:

ling unto the fayd partie. Aud the fayd Clerks of writs are authorized to graunt reple-vins and to take bond with fufficient fecuritie of the partie to profecute the Sute whofe fees fhall be for every Warrant two pence, a Replevin or Attachment three pēce, & for Bonds four pence a peece. All Attachments to be directed unto the Conftables in towns where no Marfhall is. Alfo the fayd Clerks fhal graunt Sūmons for Witneffes. [1641] *See Recorder.*

Colledge.

Wheras through the good hand of God upon us there is a Colledge founded in Cambridge in the County of Midlefex called Harvard Colledge, *for incouragement wherof this Court hath given the fumme of four hundred pounds and alfo the revenue of the Ferrie betwixt Charlftown and Bofton and that the well ordering and mannaging of the faid Colledge is of great concernment,*

Harvard Coll.

Cōmiffioners.

It is therfore ordered by this Court and Authoritie therof, That the Governour & Deputie Gover̄: for the time being and all the Magiftrates of this Jurifdiction together with the teaching Elders of the fix next adjoyning towns *viz:* Cambridge, Water-town Charlftown, Bofton, Roxburie and Dorchefter, & the Prefident of the faid Colledge for

to eftablifh or-ders.

the time being, fhal from time to time have full power & authoritie to make and eftab-lifh all fuch orders, ftatutes and conftitutions, as they fhall fee neceffary for the inftitut-ing, guiding and furthering of the faid Colledge, and feveral members therof, from time

difpofe gifts & reven.

to time, in Pietie, Moralitie & Learning, as alfo to difpofe, order and manage to the ufe and behoof of the faid Colledge and members therof, all gifts, legacyes, bequeaths, re-venues, lands and donations as either have been, are, or fhall be conferred, beftowed, or any wayes fhall fall or come to the fayd Colledge. And wheras it may come to paffe that many of the Magiftrates and faid Elders may be abfent and otherwife imployed in other weighty affairs whē the faid Colledge may need their prefent help and counfell.

power of ma-jor part.

It is therfore ordered that the greater number of Magiftrates and Elders which fhall be prefent with the Prefident, fhall have the power of the whole. Provided that if any conftitution, order or orders by them made fhall be found hurtfull unto the faid Col-

Lib: of appeal

ledg, or the members therof, or to the weal publick then upō appeal of the partie or par-ties greived, unto the company of Overfeers firft mentioned, they fhal repeal the faid or-

Power to rep.

der or orders (if they fee caufe) at their next meeting or ftand accountable therof to the next Generall court. [1636 1640 1642]

Condemned.

None exec: within 4 days

It is ordered by this Court that no man condemned to dye fhall be put to death within four dayes next after his condemnation, unles the Court fee fpeciall caufe to the

contrary

contrary, or in caſe of martial law: nor ſhall the body of any man ſo put to death be unburied twelve hours unles it be in caſe of anatomy. [1641]

Conſtables.

It is ordered by this Court, That Conſtables are to whip or puniſh any to be puniſhed by order of Authoritie (where there is not another officer appointed to doe it) in their own towns ; unles they can get another to do it.

2 It is farther ordered by the Authoritie aforeſaid, That any perſon tendered to any Conſtable of this Juriſdiction by any Conſtable or other Officer belonging to any forreign Juriſdiction in this Countrie, or by warrant from any ſuch authoritie, ſuch ſhall preſently be received, and conveyed forthwith from Conſtable to Conſtable, till they be brought unto the place to which they are ſent or before ſome Magiſtrate of this Juriſdiction who ſhall diſpoſe of them as the juſtice of the cauſe ſhall require . And that all *Hue-&-cries* ſhall be duly received and dilligently purſued to full effect. [1641] [164-]

3 It is ordered by the authoritie of this Court, That everie Conſtable within our Juriſdiction ſhall henceforth have full power to make,ſigne & put forth *Purſutes* or *Hue-&-cries* after Murtherers, Manſlayers, Peace-breakers,Theevs, Robbers,Burglarers and other Capital offenders, where no Magiſtrate is neer hand, alſo to apprehend without *Warrant,* ſuch as are overtaken with drink, ſwearing, Sabboth-breaking, lying, vagrant perſons, night-walkers, or any other that ſhall offend in any of theſe . Provided they be taken in the manner, either by ſight of the Conſtable, or by preſent informatiõ from others. As alſo to make ſearch for all ſuch perſons, either on the Sabboth day or other, when there ſhal be occaſion, in all houſes licenſed to ſell either beer or wine, or in any other ſuſpected or diſordered places, and thoſe to apprehend and keep in ſafe cuſtodie,till opportunitie ſerve to bring them before one of the next Magiſtrates for farther examination. Provided when any Conſtable is imployed by any of the Magiſtrates for apprehending of any perſon, he ſhall not doe it without *warrant* in writing, and if any perſon ſhall refuſe to aſſiſt any Conſtable in the executiõ of his office, in any of the things aforementiõed being by him required therto, they ſhal pay for neglect therof ten ſhillings, to the uſe of the Country to be levied by *warrant* from any Magiſtrate before whom any ſnch offender ſhal be brought. And if it appear by good teſtimonie, that any ſhal wilfully, obſtinately or contemptuouſly refuſe or neglect to aſſiſt any Conſtable as is before expreſſed, he ſhall pay to the uſe of the Country fourty ſhillings. And that no man may plead ignorance for ſuch neglect or refuſal, it is ordered that everie Conſtable ſhall have a black ſtaffe of five foot long, tipped at the upper end, about five inches with braſſe,as a badge of his office, which he ſhal take with him when he goeth to diſcharge any part of his office: which ſtaffe ſhall be provided at the charge of the town , and if any Magiſtrate or Conſtable or any other, upon urgent occaſion,ſhall refuſe to doe their beſt indeavours, in raiſing & proſecuting *Hue-&-cries* by foot,& if need be,by horſe,after ſuch as have cõmitted Capital crimes, they ſhall forfeit for everie ſuch offence to the uſe aforeſaid fourty ſhillings. [1646] *See In-keepers, Maſters, Oaths, Rates, Untimely death, watching.*

Conveyances fraudulent.

It is ordered by this Court and the Authoritie therof, That all covenons or fraudulent alienations or conveyances of lands, tenements or any hereditaments ſhall be of no validitie to defeat any man from due debts or legacyes, or from any juſt title, claim or poſſeſſion of that which is ſo fraudulently conveyed.

2 *For avoiding all fraudulent conveyances and that every man may know what eſtate or intereſt other men may have in any houſes,lands or other heriditamẽts they are to deal in, it is therfore ordered by the authoritie of this Court;*

That after the end of *October* 1640 no morgage, bargain, ſale, or graunt made of any houſes,lands,rents or other hereditaments where the Graunter remains in poſſeſſion, ſhall be of force againſt other perſons except the Graunter and his Heirs, unles the ſame be acknowledged before ſome Magiſtrate & recorded as is heerafter expreſſed: and that no ſuch bargain, ſale or graunt already made, in way of morgage, where the Graunter

C   remains

nor unburied 12 hours	
Conſtable correct or get another	
Forr: Juriſd: Offender conveyed frõ Cõſtable to Cõſt.	
Hue-&-cries purſued. Conſt: may put forth Hu-&-cries.	
appehend divers offenders	
ſearch for thẽ	
cõmit to cuſtodie.	
All to aſſiſt Conſt:	
on penaltie of 10 ſs.	
wilful neglect 40 ſs.	
Conſt: ſtaffe.	
Magiſtr: Conſt: &c to rayſe hu-&-crie õ Cap: offences on penal. of 40 ſs.	
Invalid.	
ũles recorded	

remains in poſſeſſion ſhall be of force againſt other but the Graunter or his Heirs, ex-

within a mõth

or 3 months

Graunter re-
fuſe to ackn:
impriſoned.

cept the ſame ſhall be entred as is heerafter expreſſed within one month after the date a-
forementioned: if the partie be within this Juriſdiction or elſe within three months after he ſhal return. And if any ſuch Graunter being required by the Grauntee, his Heirs
or Aſſignes to make ã acknowledgment of any graunt, ſale, bargain or morgage by him
made ſhall refuſe ſo to doe, it ſhall be in the power of any Magiſtrate to ſend for the
partie ſo refuſing, & commit him to priſon without *Bayle* or *Main-prize*, untill he ſhall
acknowledge the ſame, and the Grauntee is to enter his *caution* with the Recorder , and
this ſhall ſave his intereſt in the mean time. And if it be doubtfull whether it be the
deed and graunt of the partie, he ſhal be bound with Suerties to the next court of Aſſiſtants & the *caution* ſhal remain good as aforeſaid. And for recording of all ſuch graunts
ſales, bargains or morgages ; it is further ordered, that there ſhall be one appointed in

recorded in ẙ
Shire in a mõ:

& certified to
ẙ Secr: in 6
months.

everie Shire choſen by each court of the ſaid Shires for Recorders to enter all ſuch
graunts,ſales,bargains,morgages of houſes,lands, rents and other hereditamẽts as aforeſaid together with the names of Graunter and Grauntee, thing and eſtate graunted & the
date therof. All which entries ſhall be certified unto the Recorder or Secretarie for the
Generall Court within ſix months from time to time. [1640] [1641]

Councill.

*This Court conſidering how the weighty affairs of this Juriſdiction whether they con-
cern this peculiarly or have reference to the reſt of our confœderated Colonies may be duly and ſpeedily tranſacted in the vacancy of the Generall Court for the ſatisfaction of the Cõmiſſioners, in reſpect of the weighty and ſodain occaſions which may be then in hand, doth
heerby expreſſe and declare,*   That the Generall Court ought to be called by the

In caſe impor:
a Gẽeral court
called by the
Governour

ſtanding Coũ-
cil how to
be called
How many
may act for
impreſſing
men,

Governour , when the importancy of the buſines doth require it, and that time and opportunitie will ſafely admit the ſame , and that all other neceſſary matters are to be ordered and diſpatched by the major part of the Council of the Common-wealth; & therfore to that end letters ſignifying, breifly, the buſines and the time and place of meeting
for conſultation ought to be ſent unto the Aſſiſtants. Alſo it is heerby declared, that
ſeven of the ſaid Aſſiſtants meeting, the Governour or Deputy Governour being one is a
ſufficient Aſſembly to act, by impreſſing of ſoldiers or otherwiſe as need ſhall be. And
in caſe of extream and urgent neceſſitie, when indeavours are reaſonably uſed to call together the Aſſiſtants and the buſines will not admit delay, then the acts of ſo many as do

& all other
things.

aſſemble are to be accounted,and are accounted valid,& ſufficient. Alſo it is intended
that the generall words aforementioned contein in them power to impreſſe & ſend forth
ſoldiers, and all manner of victuails,veſſels at ſea,carriages and all other neceſſaries,and
to ſend *warrants* to the Treaſurer to pay for them. [1645]

Courts.

*For the better adminiſtration of juſtice and eaſing the Countrie of unneceſſary charge
and travells: it is ordered by this Court and Authoritie therof;*

4 courts of
Aſſiſtants

That there ſhal be four Quarter Courts of Aſſiſtants yearly kept by the Governour,or
Deputy Gover: and the reſt of the Magiſtrates,. the firſt of them on the firſt third day
(*viz: tuisday*) in the fourth month called *June*: the ſecond on the firſt third day of the
ſeventh month: the third on the firſt third day of the tenth mõth: the fourth on the firſt

4 Coũ: courts
at Boſton

third day of the firſt month called *March*. Alſo there be four County Courts held at
Boſton, by ſuch of the Magiſtrates as ſhall reſide in, or neer the ſame, *viz:* by any five,
four or three of them,who ſhall have power to aſſemble together upõ the laſt fift day of

for all civil
cauſ: & crim:
not extend:
to life &c

the eight, eleveneth, ſecond & fift months everie year, and there to hear & determin all
civil cauſes & criminal, not extending to life, member or baniſhment according to the
courſe of the court of Aſſiſtants, & to ſummon Juries out of the neighbour towns, & the
Marſhall & other Officers ſhall give attendance there as at other Courts . And it is fur-

4 quar: Courts
in Eſſex.

ther ordered that there ſhall be four Quarter Courts kept yearly by the Magiſtrates of
Eſſex, with ſuch other perſons of worth as ſhal frõ time to time be appointed by the General Court; at the nominatiõ of the towns in that Shire by orderly agreemẽt amõg thẽ-
ſelves, to be joyned in Commiſſion with them ſo that with the Magiſtrates they be five
in all

in all and fo that no Court be kept without one Magiftrate at the leaft: and fo to any three of the Commiffioners aforefaid may keep Court in the abfence of the reft: yet none of all the Magiftrates are excluded from any of thefe Courts who can, and pleafe to attend the fame . And the Generall Court to appoint from time to time , which of the faid Magiftrates fhall fpecially belong to everie of the faid Courts . Two of thefe Quarter Courts fhall be kept at *Salem*, the other at *Ipfwich*. The firft, the laft third day of the week in the feventh month at *Ipfwich*. The fecond at *Salem* the laft third day of the tenth month. The third at *Ipfwich* the laft third day of the firft month. The fourth the laft third day of the fourth month at *Salem*. All and every which Courts fhall be holden by the Magiftrates of *Salem* and *Ipfwich* with the reft of that County or fo many of them as fhall attend the fame; but no Jurie men fhall be warned from *Ipfwich* to *Sa-lem* nor from *Salem* to *Ipfwich*. Alfo there fhall be a Grand Jurie at either place, once a year . Which Courts fhall have the fame power in civil and criminal caufes as the courts of Affiftants have (at *Bofton*) except tryalls for life, lims or banifhment, which are who-ly referred unto the courts of Affiftants. The like libertie for County courts and tryall of caufes is granted to the Shire town of *Cambridge* for the County of *Midlefex*, as *Effex* hath, to be holden by the Magiftrates of *Midlefex* & *Suffolk* & fuch other men of worth as fhall be nominated and chofen as aforefaid, one of which Courts fhall be holden on the laft third day of the eight month , and another on the laft third day of the fecond month from year to year. And the like libertie for County Courts and tryall of caufes is granted to the County of *Norfolk* to be holden at *Salifburie* on the laft third day of the fecond month; and another at *Hampton* on fuch day as the General Court fhall appoint to be kept in each place from time to time. And if any that fhall finde himfelfe grieved with the fentence of any the faid County courts he may appeale to the next court of Affiftants. Provided he put in fufficiet *caution* according to law. Laftly, it is ordered by the Autho-ritie aforefaid that all caufes brought to the courts of Affiftants by way of appeal, and o-ther caufes fpecially belonging to the faid courts, fhall be firft determined from time to time: & that caufes of *divorce* fhall be tryed only in the faid court of Affiftants. [1635]

[1636 1639 1641 1642]

2 For the more fpeedy difpatch of all caufes which fhall concern Strangers, who cannot ftay to attend the ordinary Courts of Juftice. It is ordered by this Court and Authori-tie thereof ;

That the Governour or Deputy Governour with any two other Magiftrates, or when the Governour or Deputy Governour cannot attend it, that any three Magiftrates fhall have power to hear and determin by a Jurie of twelve men , or otherwife as is ufed in other Courts,all caufes civil and criminal triable in County Courts, which fhall arife between fuch Strangers, or wherin any fuch Stranger fhall be a partie . And all re-cords of fuch proceedings fhall be tranfmitted to the Records of the Court of Affiftants, to be entred as tryalls in other Courts, all which fhall be at the charge of the parties, as the Court fhall determin , fo as the Country be no wayes charged by fuch courts.

[1639]

3 For the electing of our Governour, Deputy Governour, Affiftants and other generall Officers upon the day or dayes appointed by our Patent to hold our yearly Court being the laft fourth day of the week (viz: Wednefday) of every Eafter Term; it is folemnly and unanimoufly decreed and eftablifhed,

That henceforth the Freemen of this Jurifdiction fhall either in perfon or by *proxie* without any *Summons* attend & confummate the Elections, at which time alfo they fhall lend their Deputies with full power to confult of and determin fuch matters as concern the welfare of this Common-wealth: from which General Court no Magiftrate or De-puty fhall depart or be difcharged without the confent of the major part both of Ma-giftrates and Deputies, during the firft four dayes of the firft Seffion thereof, under the penaltie of one hundred pounds for everie fuch default on either part. And for the after

C 2   Sefſions

Marginal notes:

not kept with-out one Magift-rate at leaft Gen: court appoint w̄ Ma-giftr: to each Court

7 mon: at Ipf-wich. 10 mo: at Salé &c:

for all civil & crim: caufes exc: cafes of life, lims, or banifhment.

Court at Cam-bridge for Midlefex.

Courts at Sa-lifburie and Hampton for Norforlk

Appeal to court of Affift

Divorce.

Courts extra-ordinary.

Courts at parryes charge

Courts of E-lection wout Summons.

No member of Court to depart wout licence.

Seſſions, if any be, the Deputies for *Dover* are at libertie whether to atſëd or not. [1643]

4 Foraſmuch as after long experience ſvee finde divers inconveniences in the manner of our proceeding in Courts by Magiſtrates and Deputies ſitting together, and account it ſviſedome to follow the laudable practice of other States, who have layd good works for go-vernment and order for iſſuing buſines of greateſt and higheſt conſequence: it is therefore or-dered by this Court and Authoritie thereof,

Gen: Court. — That henceforth the Magiſtrates may fit and act buſines by themſelves, by draw-ing up Bills and Orders which they ſhall fee good in their wiſdom, which having a-greed upon, they may preſent them to the Deputies to be conſidered of, how good and wholeſom ſuch orders are for the Countrie & accordingly to give their aſſent or diſſent. The Deputies in like manner ſitting apart by themſelves and conſulting about ſuch or-ders and laws as they in their diſcretion and experience ſhall finde meet for the common good: which agreed upon by them they may preſent to the Magiſtrates who having ſeriouſly conſidered of them may manifeſt their conſent or diſſent thereto. And when any Orders have paſſed the approbation of both Magiſtrates and Deputies, then to be ingroſſed: which in the laſt day of this Court or Seſſions ſhal be deliberately read over. Provided alſo that all matters of Judicature which this Court ſhall take cognizance of, ſhall be iſſued in like manner (unles the Court upon ſome particular occaſion or buſines agree otherwiſe). [1644]

Magiſtrates act apart.

Bils read over ý laſt day of the Seſſion, Matter of Ju-dicature

Criminal cauſes.
It is ordered by this court & Authoritie thereof, That everie man that is to anſwer for any criminal cauſe, whether he be in priſon or under *Bayle* his cauſe ſhall be heard and determined at the next Court that hath proper cognizance thereof and may be done without prejudice of juſtice. [1641] *See Courts, Lib: com: Puniſhment, Torture.*

heard next Court

Crueltie.
It is ordered by this Court and Authoritie thereof; That no man ſhall exerciſe any tyranny or cruelty towards any bruit creatures which are uſually kept for the uſe of man. [1641]

Damages pretended.
It is ordered by this Court and Authoritie thereof; That no man in any Sute or Ac-tion againſt another ſhall fally pretend great damages or debts to vex his adverſary, and if it ſhall appear any doth ſo, the Court ſhall have power to ſet a reaſonable fine on his head. [1641]

Finable.

Death untimely.
It is ordered by this Court and Authoritie thereof; That whenſoever any perſon ſhall come to any very ſodain, untimely or unnatural death, ſome Affiſtant or the Conſta-ble of that town ſhall forthwith ſummon a Jurie of twelve diſcreet men to inquire of the cauſe and manner of their death, who ſhall preſent a true verdict thereof, to ſome neer Affiſtant, or to the next court (to be holden for that Shire) upon their oath. [1641]

Tryed by in-queſt.

Deeds and writings.
It is ordered by this court and Authoritie thereof; That no conveyance, deed or promiſe whatſoever ſhall be of validitie , if it be gotten by illegal violence, impriſon-ment, threatening or any kinde of forcible compulſion, called *Dures.* [1641]

Invalid.

Deputies for the Generall Court.
For eaſing the body of Freemen now increaſing, and better diſpatching the buſines of Generall Courts, It is ordered and by this Court declared;

That henceforth it ſhall be lawfull for the Freemen of everie Plantation to chooſe their Deputies before every Generall Court, to confer of, and prepare ſuch publick bu-ſines as by them ſhall be thought fit to conſider of at the next Generall court. And that ſuch perſons as ſhall be heerafter ſo deputed by the Freemen of the ſeverall Plantations to deal on their behalfe in the publick affairs of the Common-wealth, ſhall have the full power and voices of all the ſaid Freemen derived to them for the making and eſtabliſh-ing of Laws, granting of lands, and to deal in all other affairs of the Comon-wealth wherin

Towns chooſe Deputies.

their power before the Court

their power in Court

wherein the Freemen have to doe: the matter of election of Magiftrates and other Officers only excepted wherin every Freeman is to give his own voice. [1634]

margin: matter of election except:

2 *Forasmuch as through the bleffing of God the number of towns are much increafed,*

It is therefore ordered and by this Court enacted;

margin: Nùber of Dep: for each town.

That henceforth no town fhall fend more then two Deputies to the General Court; though the number of Freemen in any town be more then twenty . And that all towns which have not to the number of twenty Freemen fhall fend but one Deputy, & fuch towns as have not ten Freemen fhall fend none , but fuch Freemen fhall vote with the next town in the choice of their Deputie or Deputies til this Court take further order. [1636 1638]

margin: Deputies may fettle differ: a-bout elect: of Deputies & order their own body.

3 It is ordered by this Court and Authoritie therof, That when the Deputyes for feverall towns are met together before, or at any General court, it fhall be lawfull for them or the major part of them to hear and determin any difference that may arife about the election of any of their members, and to order things amongft themfelves that may concern the well ordering of their body . And that hearafter the Deputies for the General court fhall be elected by papers as the Governour is chofen. [1634 1635]

margin: Where cho-fen. How qualified.

4 It is ordered by this Court and Authoritie therof; That the Freemen of any Shire or town have liberty to choofe fuch Deputies for the General court either in their own Shire, Town, or elfewhere, as they judge fitteft, fo be it they be Freemen and inhabiting within this Jurifdiction. And becaufe wee cannot forefee what variety and weight of occafions may fall into future confideration, & what counfells we may ftand in need of: wee decree that the Deputies to attend the General court in the behalfe of the Coü-try fhall not at any time be ftated and enacted but from court to court, or at the moft but for one year, that the Countrie may have an annual liberty to doe in that cafe what is moft behoofefull for the beft welfare therof. [1641]

margin: Stated but for one year at moft.

Diftreffe.

It is ordered by this Court and Authoritie therof, That no mans corn or hay that is in the field or upon the cart, nor his garden-ftuffe, nor any thing fubject to prefent decay fhall be taken in any diftreffe, unles he that takes it doth prefently beftow it where it may not be imbeazled nor fuffer fpoyl or decay, or give fecuritie to fatisfie the worth therof if it comes to any harm. [1641]

margin: Secured.

Dowries.

Forafmuch as no provifion hath yet been made for any certain maintainance for Wives after the death of their Husbands, be it ordered and enacted by this prefent Court and Authoritie therof;

That every married Woman (living with her Husband in this Jurifdiction or other where abfent from him with his confent or through his meer default, or inevitable pro-vidence, or in cafe of divorce where fhe is the innocent partie) that fhal not before mar-riage be eftated by way of joynture in fome houfes, lands, tenements or other hereditamments for term of her life, fhall immediatly after the death of her Husband have right and intereft by way of *dower,* in, and to one third part of all fuch houfes, lands, tenements, rents and hereditaments as her faid Husband was feized of, to his own ufe, either in pof-feffion, reverfion or remainder in any eftate of inheritance (or *franc-tenement* not then de-termined) at any time during the marriage to have and injoy for term of her na-tural life according to the eftate of fuch Husband free, and freely difcharged of and from all titles, debts, rents, charges, judgements, executions and other incumbran-ces whatfoever had, made, or fuffered by her faid Husband during the faid mar-riage between them ; or by any other perfon claiming by, from, or under him otherwife then by any act or confent of fuch Wife , as the laws of this Court fhall ratefie and allow: and if the Heir of the Husband or other perfon inter-efted, fhall not within one month after lawfull demand made , affigne and fet out to

margin: What wives are dowable

margin: wherof.

margin: for life.

margin: free of incum-brance.

C 3

How to be af-signed.

out to fuch widow, her juft third part with conveniencie or to her fatisfaction according to the intent of this Law, then upõ a *writ* of *dower* in the court of that Shire where
the faid houfes, lands, tenements or other hereditaments fhall lye; or in the court of
Affiftants (if the fame lye in feverall Shires) her *dower* or third part fhall be affigned her to
be fet forth in feverall by mets and bounds, by fuch perfons as the fame Court fhall ap-

with cofts & damages. Limitation

point for that purpofe, with all cofts and damages fufteined. Provided alwayes that
this Law fhall not extend to any houfes lands, tenements or other hereditaments folde or
conveyed away, by any husband *bona fide* for valuable confideration, before the laft of
the ninth month now laft paft. And it is farther inacted that everie fuch Wife as is before expreffed immediatly after the death of her Husband, fhall have intereft in, and unto

Third of per-fonal eftate

one third part of all fuch monie, goods and chattels, real and perfonal of what kinde foe-
ver as her Husband fhall dye poffeffed of (fo much as fhall be fufficient for the difcharge
of his Funerall and juft debts being firft deducted) to be allowed and fet out to her as is
heer before appointed for her Dowrie. Provided alwayes that every fuch widow fo

reftreint from waft.

endowed as aforefaid fhall not commit or fuffer any ftrip or waft, but fhall maintain all
fuch houfes, fences and inclofures as fhall be affigned to her for her Dowrie, and fhall
leave the fame in good and fufficient reparations in all points. [1647]

Drovers.

It is ordered by this Court and Authoritie therof; That if any man fhall have occafion to lead or drive cattle from place to place that is far off, fo that they be weary or

Liberty.

hungrie, or fall fick or lame, it fhall be lawfull to reft and refrefh them for a competent
time in any open place that is not corn, meadow, or inclofed for fome particular ufe.

[1641]

Ecclefiasticall:

1 All the people of God within this Jurisdiction who are not in a Church way and be
orthodox in judgement and not fcandalous in life fhall have full libertie to gather themfelves into a Church eftate, provided they doe it in a chriftian way with due obfervation of the rules of Chrift revealed in his word. Provided alfo that the General Court
doth not, nor will heerafter approve of any fuch companyes of men as fhall joyne in any

Approbation.

pretended way of Church fellowfhip unles they fhall acquaint the Magiftrates and the
Elders of the neighbour Churches where they intend to joyn, & have their approbation
therin .

Non-approba:

2 And it is farther ordered , that no perfon being a member of any Church which
fhall be gathered without the approbation of the Magiftrates and the faid Churches fhal
be admitted to the Freedom of this Common-wealth.

Ordinances

3 Everie Church hath free liberty to exercife all the Ordinances of God according to
the rules of the Scripture.

Officers.

4 Everie Church hath free libertie of election and ordination of all her Officers from
time to time. Provided they be able, pious and orthodox.

Members,

5 Everie Church hath alfo free libertie of admiffion, recommendation, difmiffion &
expulfion or depofall of their Officers and members upon due caufe, with free exercife of
the difciplin and cenfures of Chrift according to the rules of his word.

No humane Ordinances.

6 No injunction fhall be put upon any Church, church Officer or member in point
of doctrine, worfhip or difciplin, whether for fubftance or circumftance befides the in-
ftitutions of the Lord.

Fafts & Feafts

7 Everie Church of Chrift hath freedom to celebrate dayes of Fafting and prayer and
of Thankfgiving according to the word of God.

Elders meet:

8 The Elders of churches alfo have libertie to meet monthly, quarterly or otherwife
in convenient numbers and places, for conference and confultations about chriftian and
church queftions and occafions.

Members üder civil juftice.

9 All Churches alfo have libertie to deal with any their members in a church way
that are in the hands of juftice, fo it be not to retard and hinder the courfe therof.

10 Everie

10 Everie Church hath libertie to deal with any Magiftrate, Deputy of court, or o-
ther Officer whatfoever that is a member of theirs , in a church way in cafe of apparent
and juft offence, given in their places, fo it be done with due obfervance and refpect. civil Officers.

11 Wee alfo allow private meetings for edification in Religion amongft chriftians of
all forts of people fo it be without juft offence , both for number, time, place and other
circumftances . Private meet:

12 *For the preventing and removing of errour and offence that may grow and fpread in*
any of the Churches in this Jurisdiction, and for the preferving of truth & peace in the fe-
verall Churches within themfelves, and for the maintainance and exercife of brotherly cõ-
munion amongft all the Churches in the country.

It is allowed and ratified by the authoritie of this Court, as a lawfull libertie of the
Churches of Chrift, that once in every month of the year (when the feafon will bear it) Monthly meet ings.
it fhall be lawfull for the Minifters and Elders of the Churches neer adjoyning, together
with any other of the Brethren, with the confent of the Churches, to affemble by courfe
in everie feveral church one after another , to the intent, that after the preaching of the For preaching & conference
word, by fuch a Minifter as fhal be requefted therto, by the Elders of the Church where
the Affemby is held, the reft of the day may be fpent in publick chriftian conference,
about the difcuffing and refolving of any fuch doubts & cafes of confcience concerning
matter of doctrine, or worfhip, or government of the Church as fhall be propounded by
any of the Brethren of that Church; with leave alfo to any other Brother to propound
his objections, or anfwers, for further fatiffaction according to the word of God. Provided that the whole action be guided and moderated by the Elders of the Church where Moderators.
the Affembly is held, or by fuch others as they fhall appoint. And that nothing be
concluded & impofed by way of Authoritie from one, or more Churches, upon another, No Prefbyte-rial authority over Chur:
but only by way of brotherly conference & confultations , that the truth may be fearch-
ed out to the fatisfying of every mans confcience in the fight of God according to his
word. And becaufe fuch an Affemblie and the work therof cannot be duly attended if
other Lectures be held the fame week, it is therfore agreed with the confent of the
Churches, that in what week fuch an Affembly is held all the Lectures in all the neigh- no Lectures ỹ week.
bouring Churches for the week dayes fhall be forborne, that fo the publick fervice of
Chrift in this Affembly may be tranfacted with greater diligence & attention. [1641]

13 *Forafmuch as the open contempt of Gods word and Meffengers therof is the defolat-*
ing finne of civil States and Churches and that the preaching of the word by thofe whom
God doth fend, is the chief ordinary means ordained of God for the converting, edifying
and faving the foules of the Elect through the prefence and power of the Holy-Ghoft, ther-
unto promifed: and that the miniftry of the word, is fet up by God in his Churches, for
thofe holy ends: and according to the refpect or contempt of the fame and of thofe whom
God hath fet apart for his own work & imployment, the weal or woe of all Chriftian States
is much furthered and promoted; it is therfore ordered and decreed,

That if any chriftian (fo called) within this Jurisdiction fhall contemptuoufly behave himfelfe toward the Word preached or the Meffengers therof called to difpenfe contempt of the word &c
the fame in any Congregation; when he doth faithfully execute his Service and Office
therin, according to the will and word of God, either by interrupting him in his preaching , or by charging him falfely with any errour which he hath not taught in the open
face of the Church: or like a fon of *Korah* caft upon his true doctrine or himfelfe any
reproach, to the difhonour of the Lord Jefus who hath fent him and to the difparagement of that his holy Ordinance, and making Gods wayes contemptible and ridicu-
lous: that everie fuch perfon or perfons (whatfoever cenfure the Church may paffe)
fhall for the firft fcandall be convented and reproved openly by the Magiftrate at firft offence openly reprov ed &c:
fome Lecture, and bound to their good behaviour. And if a fecond time they Second offen:
break forth into the like contemptuous carriages , they fhall either pay five pounds
to the publick Treafurie; or ftand two hours openly upon a block or ftool, four foot
high

high on a lecture day with a paper fixed on his breaſt, written in Capital letters [AN O-PEN AND OBSTINATE CONTEMNER OF GODS HOLY ORDINANCES] that others may fear and be aſhamed of breaking out into the like wickednes. [1646]

14 It is ordered and decreed by this Court and Authoritie therof; That wherefoeve the miniſtry of the word is eſtabliſhed according to the order of the Goſpell throughout this Juriſdiction every perfon ſhall duly reſort and attend therunto reſpectively upon the Lords days & upon ſuch publick Faſt dayes, & dayes of Thankſgiving as are to be generally kept by the appointmẽt of Authoritie: & if any perfon withĩ this Juriſdictiõ ſhal without juſt and neceſſarie cauſe withdraw himſelfe frõ hearing the publick miniſtry of the word after due meanes of conviction uſed, he ſhall forfeit for his abſence from everie ſuch publick meeting five ſhillings. All ſuch offences to be heard and determined by any one Magiſtrate or more from time to time. [1646]

15 *Forafmuch as the peace and profperity of Churches and members therof as well as ci-vil Rights & Liberties are carefully to be maintained, it is ordered by this Court & decreed,* That the civil Authoritie heer eſtabliſhed hath power and liberty to ſee the peace, ordinances and rules of Chriſt be obſerved in everie Church according to his word. As alſo to deal with any church-member in a way of civil juſtice notwithſtanding any church relation, office, or intereſt; ſo it be done in a civil and not in an eccleſiaſtical way. Nor ſhall any church cenſure degrade or depoſe any man from any civil dignity, office or authoritie he ſhall have in the Common-wealth. [1641]

16 *Forafmuch as there are many Inhabitants in divers towns, who leave their feveral habitations and therby draw much of the in-come of their eſtates into other towns wherby the miniſtry is much neglected, it is therfore ordered by this Court and the authoritie therof;* That from henceforth all lands, cattle and other eſtates of any kinde whatfoever, ſhall be lyable to be rated to all cõmon charges whatfoever, either for the Church, Town or Cõmon-wealth in the ſame place where the eſtate is from time to time. And to the end there may be a convenient habitation for the uſe of the miniſtry in everie town in this Juriſdiction to remain to poſterity. It is decreed by the authoritie of this Court that where the major part of the Inhabitants (according to the order of regulating valid town acts) ſhall graunt, build, or purchaſe ſuch habitation it ſhall be good in law, and the particular ſum upon each perſon aſſeſſed by juſt rate, ſhal be duly paid according as in other caſes of town rates. Provided alwayes that ſuch graunt, deed of purchaſe and the deed of gift therupon to the uſe of a preſent preaching Elder and his next ſucceſſour and ſo from time to time to his ſucceſſors: be entred in the town book and acknowledged before a Magiſtrate, and recorded in the Shire court. [1647] *See charges publ: fec: 3.*

Elections.

It is ordered by this Court and Authoritie therof: That for the yearly chooſing of Aſſiſtants for the time to come in ſtead of papers the Freemen ſhall uſe indian corn and beans. the indian corn to manifeſt election, the beans for blanks. And that if any Freeman ſhall put in more then one indian corn or bean for the choiſe or refuſal of any publick Officer, he ſhall forfeit for everie ſuch offence ten pounds. And that any man that is not free or otherwiſe hath not libertie of voting, putting in any vote ſhal forfeit the like ſum of ten pounds. [1643]

2 *For the preventing of many inconveniences that otherwife may arife upon the yearly day of Election, and that the work of that day may be the more orderly, eafily and fpeedily iffued, it is ordered by this Court and the authoritie therof.*

That the Freemen in the ſeveral towns and villages within this Juriſdiction, ſhall this next year from time to time either in perfon or by proxie ſealed up, make all their elections, by papers, indian corn and beans as heerafter is expreſſed, to be taken, ſealed up, & ſent to the court of Election as this order appoints, the Governour, Deputie Governour, Major Generall, Treaſurer, Secretary and Cõmiſſioners for the united Colonies to be choſen by writing, open or once folded, not twiſted or rolled up, that ſo they may be

---

Margin notes:

Abſence from church Aſſem:

fined 5 ſs

Civil author: may preſerve peace in chu: Puniſh chur: members nor ſhal chur: cenſ: diſanul civil dignity.

What is ratable for the miniſtry.

Miniſters houſ

to go to ſucceſſors.

recorded.

Election by indian corn & beans. no man put in above one, on penal: of 10 li.

no non-Frem: any, on like penaltie.

Election by proxies how to be carried

be the fooner and furer perufed: and all the Affiftants to be chofen by indian corn and beans, the indian corn to manifeft election as in *Sect:* 1: and for fuch fmall villages as come not in perfon and that fend no Deputies to the Court, the Conftable of the faid village, together with two or three of the chiefe Freemen fhall receive the votes of the reft of their Freemen, and deliver them together with their own fealed up to the Deputie or Deputies for the next town, who fhall carefully convey the fame unto the faid Court of Election. [1647]

Small villages to joyn w̃ next towns.

    3 *Forafmuch as the choice of Affiftants in cafe of fupply is of great concernment, and with all care and circumfpection to be attended; It is therfore ordered by this Court and Authoritie therof,*

    That when any Affiftants are to be fupplyed, the Deputies for the General Court fhall give notice to their Conftables or Select men to call together their Freemen in their feverall towns: to give in their votes unto the number of feven perfons, or as the General Court fhall direct, who fhall then and there appoint one to carrie them fealed up unto their Shire towns upon the laft fourth day of the week in the firft month from time to time; which perfons for each town fo affembled fhall appoint one for each Shire to carrie them unto *Boston* the fecond third day of the fecond month there to be opened before two Magiftrates. And thofe feven or other number agreed upon as aforefaid, that have moft votes fhall be the men which fhall be nominated at the court of Election for Affiftants as aforefaid. Which perfons the Agents for each Shire fhall forthwith fignifie to the Conftables of all their feveral towns in writing under their hands with the number of votes for each perfon: all which the faid Conftables fhall forthwith fignifie to their Freemen. And as any hath more votes then other fo fhall they be put to vote. [1647]

Affiftants fupplyed

by vote fealed up:

opened at Bofton

fignified to y̆ Freemen.

    4 It is decreed and by this Court declared That it is the conftant libertie of the Freemen of this Jurisdiction to choofe yearly at the court of Election out of the Freemen, all the general Officers of this Jurisdiction, and if they pleafe to difcharge them at the court of Election by way of vote they may doe it without fhewing caufe. But if at any other General Court, we hold it due juftice that the reafon therof be alledged and proved. By general Officers we mean our Governour, Deputy Governour, Affiftants, Treafurer, General of our wars, our Admirall at fea, Commiffioners for the united-Colonies and fuch others as are, or heerafter may be of the like general nature. [1641] *See courts Sect:* 3.

Gen: officers [chofen how [[difcharg ed.

Explainat: of gen: Officers.

<h3 style="text-align:center">Efcheats.</h3>

    It is ordered by this Court and Authoritie therof, That where no Heir or Owner of houfes, lands, tenements, goods or chattels can be found: they fhall be feized to the publick Treafurie till fuch Heirs or owners fhall make due claim therto, unto whom they fhall be reftored upon juft and reafonable terms. [1646]

<h3 style="text-align:center">Farms.</h3>

    It is ordered by this Court and Authoritie therof, That all Farms which are within the bounds of any town fhall henceforth be of the fame town in which they lye, except *Meadford.* [1641] *See militarie. fee watches.*

<h3 style="text-align:center">Fayrs & Markets.</h3>

    It is ordered by the Authoritie of this Court that there fhall henceforth be a Market kept at *Boston* in the county of *Suffolk* upõ the fift day of the week from time to time. And at *Salem* in the county of *Effex* upon the fourth day of the week from time to time. And at *Lyn* on the third day of the week from time to time. And at *Charls-town* in the county of *Middlefex* upon the fixt day of the week from time to time. It is alfo ordered and heerby graunted unto *Salem* afore-mentioned to have two Fayrs in a year on the laft fourth day of the third month and the laft fourth day of the feventh month from year to year. Alfo *Water-town* in the County of *Middlefex* is graunted two Fayrs on the firft fixt day of the fourth month & the firft fixt day of the feventh month from year to year. Alfo *Dorchefter* in the County of *Suffolk* is graunted two Fayrs on the third

At Bofton.

Salem. Charls-town.

Two Fayrs a year at Salem.

Water-town.

Dorchefter.

D

fourth

fourth day of the firſt month and the laſt fourth day of the eight month from year to year [1633 1634 1636 1638]

Ferries.

For ſetling all common ferries in a right courſe both for the Paſſengers and Owners, it is ordered by this Court and authoritie therof;

Priviledge of Ferries. That whoſoever hath a Ferry graunted upon any paſſage ſhall have the ſole libertie for tranſporting paſſengers from the place where ſuch Ferrie is graunted, to any other ferrie-place where ferrie-boats uſe to land, and any ferrie-boat that ſhall land paſſengers at any other Ferrie may not take paſſengers from thence if the ferrie-boat of the place be ready. **Men may paſſ in own or neighbours boat.** Provided this order ſhall not prejudice the libertie of any that do uſe to paſſe in their own or neighbours *cannooes* or boats to their ordinary labour or buſines. **Double pay in the night** Alſo Ferrimen are allowed to take double pay at ſuch common Ferries after day light is done, and thoſe that make not preſent pay, being required, ſhall give their names in writing or a pawn to the Ferriman, **How Ferrymē may recover their pay.** or elſe he may complain of ſuch before a Magiſtrate to get ſatisfaction. **Magiſtr: and Dep: paſſage free:** And it is ordered that all the Magiſtrates and ſuch as are, or from time to time ſhall be choſen to ſerve as Deputies of the General Court, with their neceſſary attendants *viz:* a man and a horſe at all times, during the time of their being Magiſtrates or Deputies [and not their whole families] ſhall be paſſage-free over all Ferries. **payd by the Countrie for them & others 6 li. per añ:** Provided where Ferries are appropriated to any, or rented out & ſo be out of the Countries hands their paſſage ſhall be paid by the Countrie. And the Ferrimen of *Charls-River* are allowed for the paſſage of the Magiſtrates, Deputies, Grand and petty Juriemen, priſoners; Keepers and Marſhals, by agreemenr with them ſix pounds *per annum* to be paid by the Treaſurer.

And wheras men doe paſſe over the common Ferries in great danger oftentimes, and the Ferrimen excuſe themſelves by the importunitie of paſſengers and want of law to inable them to keep due order touching paſſengers, its therfore heerby farther ordered;

Secur: paſſen: That no perſon ſhall preſſe or enter into any ferrie-boat contrary to the will of the Ferriman or of the moſt of the paſſengers firſt entred upon payn of ten ſhillings for every ſuch attempt: and that everie Ferriman that ſhall permit and allow any perſon to come into his boat againſt the will of any of the Magiſtrates or Deputies or any of the Elders ſhipped in ſuch boat or the greater part of the paſſengers in the ſaid boat, ſhall forfeit for everie perſon ſo admitted or received againſt ſuch their will ſo declared the ſum of twentie ſhillings. **Ferriman's power.** And it ſhall be in the power of any of the Ferrimen to keep out or put out of his boat any perſon that ſhall preſſe, enter into, or ſtay in any ſuch ferrie-boat contrary to this Order. And it is farther ordered that all perſons ſhall be received into ſuch ferrie-boats according to their comming, firſt or laſt, only all Publick **men ſhall paſſe as they come exc: publick perſons &c:** perſons or ſuch as goe upon publick or urgent occaſions, as Phiſitians, Chirurgeons and Midwives and ſuch other as are called to woemens labours, ſuch ſhall be tranſported with the firſt. [1641 1644 1646 1647] *See Colledge.*

Fines.

Wheras divers perſons indebted to the Countrie for publick Rates, & others for Fines who for avoiding payment ſomtime ſell their houſes and lands, and ſend away their goods to other Plantations, it is therfore ordered by the authoritie of this Court,

where no eſt: is foūd perſon attached. That the Treaſurer ſhall graunt *Warrant* to the Marſhall to attach the bodyes of ſuch perſons, & keep them til they make ſatisfaction; and all ſuch perſons as are to pay any fines if they have not lands or goods to be diſtreined ſhall have their bodyes attach- **The court may diſch: from priſon.** ed to make ſatisfaction. Provided that any Court of Aſſiſtants or County Court may diſcharge any ſuch perſon from impriſonment if they ſhall finde them indeed unable to make ſatisfaction. [1638]

Fyre.

In what caſes he y̆ kindles fire ſhal pay all damages It is ordered by this Court and the Authoritie therof, that whoſoever ſhall kindle any fyres in woods or grounds lying in common or incloſed, ſo as the ſame ſhall run into ſuch corn grounds or incloſures; before the tenth of the firſt month or after the laſt of the ſecond month, or on the laſt day of the week, or on the Lords day ſhall pay all damages and

and half ſo much for a Fine , or if not able to pay then to be corporally puniſhed by *Warrant* from one Magiſtrate or the next County Court as the offence ſhall deſerve, not exceeding twenty ſtripes for one offence . Provided that any man may kindle fyre in his own ground at any time , ſo as no damage come therby either to the Country or any particular perſon . And whoſoever ſhall wittingly and willingly burn or deſtroy any frame, timber hewed, ſawn or ryven, heaps of wood, charcoal, corn, hay, ſtraw, hemp or flax he ſhall pay double damages.

and be fined or corporally puniſhed

Wilfull burning timber, co &c: double damage

Fiſh. Fiſher-men.

U PON *the petition of the Inhabitants of* Marble-head *this Court doth heerby declare that howſoever it hath been an allowed cuſtom for forreign fiſhermen to make uſe of ſuch Harbours and Grounds in this Countrie as have not been inhabited by Engliſh men, and to take timber and wood at their pleaſure for all their occaſions , yet in theſe parts which are now poſſeſſed and the lands diſpoſed in proprietie unto ſeverall towns and perſons and that by his Majeſtyes graunt under the Great Seal of England,*

Forr: Fiſhermens cuſtom for timber &c:

It is not now lawfull for any perſon either Fiſherman or other , either Forreiner or of this Countrie to enter upon the lands ſo appropriated to any town or perſon, or to take any wood or timber in any ſuch place without the licence of ſuch town or Proprietor : and if any perſon ſhall treſpaſſe heerin the Town or Proprietor ſo injured may take their remedie by Action at law , or may preſerve their goods or other interreſt by oppoſing lawfull force againſt ſuch unjuſt violence . Provided that it ſhall be lawfull for ſuch Fiſhermen as ſhall be imployed by any Inhabitants in this Juriſdiction in the ſeverall ſeaſons of the year to make uſe of any of our Harbours and ſuch lands as are neer adjoyning, for the drying of their fiſh or other needfull occaſions , as alſo to have ſuch timber or fire-wood as they ſhall have neceſſary uſe of for their fiſhing ſeaſons where it may be ſpared , ſo as they make due ſatisfaction for the ſame to ſuch Town or Proprietor. [1646]

not allowed.

Lib: for our own Fiſhermē

upon due ſatisfaction.

Forgerie.

I T is ordered by this Court and Authoritie therof, That if any perſon ſhall forge any Deed or conveyance, Teſtament, Bond, Bill, Releaſ, Acquittance, Letter of Attourny or any writing to pervert equitie and juſtice, he ſhall ſtand in the *Pillory* three ſeverall Lecture dayes and render double damages to the partie wronged and alſo be diſſabled to give any evidence or verdict to any Court or Magiſtrate. [1646]

Fornication.

I T is ordered by this Court and Authoritie therof , That if any man ſhall commit Fornication with any ſingle woman , they ſhall be puniſhed either by enjoyning to Marriage , or Fine, or corporall puniſhment, or all or any of theſe as the Judges in the courts of Aſſiſtants ſhall appoint moſt agreeable to the word of God. And this Order to continue till the Court take further order. [1642]

Freemen, Non-Freemen.

W HERAS *there are within this Juriſdiction many members of Churches who to exempt themſelves from all publick ſervice in the Common-wealth will not come in, to be made Freemen , is is therfore ordered by this Court and the Authoritie therof,*

That all ſuch members of Churches in the ſeverall towns within this Juriſdiction ſhall not be exempted from ſuch publick ſervice as they are from time to time choſen to by the Freemen of the ſeverall towns; as Conſtables, Jurors, Select-men and Surveyors of high-wayes. And if any ſuch perſon ſhall refuſe to ſerve in, or take upon him any ſuch Office being legally choſen therunto, he ſhall pay for every ſuch refuſall ſuch Fine as the town ſhall impoſe, not exceeding twenty ſhillings as Freemen are lyable to in ſuch caſes. [1647]

Who are compellable to publ: ſervices

Fugitives , Strangers.

I T is ordered by this Court and Authoritie therof, That if any people of other nations profeſſing the true Chiſtian Religion ſhall flee to us from the tyrañie or oppreſſion of their perſecutors , or from Famine, Wars, or the like neceſſarie and

D 2compulſarie

Harboured.	compulfarie caufe , they fhall be entertained and fuccoured amongft us according to that power and prudence God fhall give us. [1641]

Gaming.

UPON *complaint of great diforder by the ufe of the game called* Shuffle-board, *in houfes of common entertainment, wherby much pretious time is fpent unfruitfully and much waft of wine and beer occafioned, it is therfore ordered and enacted by the Authoritie of this Court;*

Shuffleboard penalties. No gaming for mony on pen: of treble value.	That no perfon fhall henceforth ufe the faid game of Shuffle-board in any fuch houfe , nor in any other houfe ufed as common for fuch purpofe, upon payn for every Keeper of fuch houfe to forfeit for every fuch offence twenty fhillings : and for every perfon playing at the faid game in any fuch houfe, to forfeit for everie fuch offence five fhillings : Nor fhall any perfon at any time play or game for any monie, or mony-worth upon penalty of forfeiting treble the value therof : one half to the partie in-forming , the other half to the Treafurie. And any Magiftrate may hear and deter-min any offence againft this Law. [1646 1647]

Generall Court.

Who have power to Re-prive. to pardon.	IT is ordered , and by this Court declared that the Governour and Deputie Gover-nour joyntly confenting , or any three Affiftants concurring in confent fhall have power out of Court to reprive a condemned malefactor till the next Court of Affiftants: or Generall Court . And that the General Court only fhall have power to pardon a condemned malefactor.
None free frõ forrein Am-baffie, that accepts the fervice.	Alfo it is declared that the General Court hath libertie and Authoritie to fend forth any member of this Common-wealth , of what qualitie and condition or office whatfo-ever into forrein parts , about any publick Meffage or negociation : notwithftanding any office or relation whatfoever. Provided the partie fo fent be acquainted with the affairs he goeth about, and be willing to undertake the fervice .
Major part in Gen: Court diffolve or adjourn·	Nor fhall any General Court be diffolved or adjourned without the confent of the major part therof . [1641] *See Counfell, Courts.*

Governour.

A cafting vote in the Gover: and Prefid: in Courts &.	IT is ordered, and by this Court declared that the Governour fhall have a cafting vote whenfoever an *equivote* fhall fall out in the Court of Affiftants , or general Affemblie: fo fhall the Prefident or Moderatour have in all civil Courts or Affemblies [1641] *See Gen: Court.*

Herefie.

ALTHOUGH *no humane power be Lord over the Faith & Confciences of men, and therfore may not conftrein them to beleive or profeffe againft their Confciences : yet becaufe fuch as bring in damnable herefies, tending to the fubverfion of the Chriftian Faith, and deftruction of the foules of men, ought duly to be reftreined from fuch notorious im-piety , it is therfore ordered and decreed by this Court;*

	That if any Chriftian within this Jurisdiction fhall go about to fubvert and de-ftroy the chriftian Faith and Religion , by broaching or mainteining any damnable herefie ; as denying the immortalitie of the Soul, or the refurrection of the body , or any fin to be repented of in the Regenerate , or any evil done by the outward man to be accounted fin: or denying that Chrift gave himfelf a Ranfom for our fins , or fhal affirm that wee are not juftified by his Death and Righteoufnes , but by the perfection of our own works ; or fhall deny the moralitie of the fourth commandement, or fhall indeavour to feduce others to any the herifies aforementioned , everie fuch perfon con-
Bañifhment.	tinuing obftinate therin after due means of conviction fhall be fentenced to Bañifh-ment. [1646]

Hydes & Skins.

WHERAS *fome perfons more feeking their own private advantage then the good of the publick doe tranfport raw hydes & pelts, it is ordered and by this Court enacted,*

Raw hides.	That henceforth no perfon fhall deliver aboard any fhip or other veffell , direct-ly or indirectly any raw hyde, skin, pelt or leather unwrought with intent to have the fame

fame tranfported out of this Jurifdiction upon pain to forfeit the fame or the value
therof . 　 And that no Mafter of any fhip or veffel fhall receive any raw hyde , skin, Forfeit.
pelt , or leather unwrought directly or indirectly, aboard his fhip or veffel to be fo
tranfported upon the like penalty . 　 Provided that any perfon ftranger or other may
tranfport any hydes or skins brought hither from beyond the feas by way of Merchan-
dize , or the skins of Beaver, Moof, Bear and Otter. [1646]

Hygh-wayes.

*TO the end there may be convenient high-wayes for Travellers, it is ordered by the
Authoritie of this Court;*

That all common high-wayes fhall be fuch as may be moft eafie, and fafe for travellers : 　 to which purpofe everie town (where any fuch high-way is made, or to be
made) fhall appoint two or three men of the next town, whofe Inhabitants have moft By whom
layd out.
occafion therof, chofen & appointed by their faid town, who fhal from time to time lay
out all common high-wayes where they may be moft convenient ; notwithftanding Places ex-
empted.
any mans proprietie, (fo as it occafion not the pulling down of any mans houfe , or laying open any garden or orchard): 　 who in common grounds or where the foyle is wet,
myrie , or verie rockie fhall lay out fuch high-wayes the wyder , *viz:* fix, eight, ten or
more rods .

Provided that if any man be therby damaged in his improved ground the town Recompence
to Propriet:
fhall make him reafonable fatisfaction by eftimation of thofe of the two towns that layd
out the fame . 　 And if fuch perfons deputed cannot agree in either cafe it fhall be referred to the County Court of that Shire ; 　 or to the Court of Affiftants who fhall have
power to hear and determin the Cafe . 　 And if any perfon finde himfelfe juftly grieved with any act or thing done by the perfons deputed aforefaid : 　 he may appeal to the Appeal.
County Court aforefaid, or to the Court of Affiftants , 　 but if he be found to complain
without caufe he fhall furely pay all charges of the parties and Court during that Action
and alfo be fined to the Countrie as the Court fhall adjudge. [1639]

2 It is ordered and declared by this Court that the felected Townf-men of everie
town have power to lay out (by themfelves or others) particular and private wayes Private wayes
in towns.
concerning their own town only : 　 fo as no damage be done to any man without
due recompence to be given by the judgement of the faid Townf-men, and one or
two chofen by the faid Townf-men and one or two chofen by the partie : 　 and if any
man fhall finde himfelfe juftly greived he may appeal to the next County Court of that
Shire who fhall doe juftice therin on both hands as in other cafes of appeals. [1642]

3 　 *UPON information that divers high-wayes are much annoyed and incumbred by
gates and rayls erected upon them , it is ordered and enacted by the Authoritie
of this Court ,*

That upon any information or complaint made either to the court of Affiftants,
or any County Court or to any Magiftrate of any fuch gates or rayls erected, or to be One Magiftr:
power to or-
der redreffe
erected upon any common high-way , the fame Court or Magiftrate fhall appoint a
Committee of difcreet and indifferent men to view fuch incumbrance, and to order the
reformation therof . 　 And if the parties whom it fhall concern fhall not fubmit to
fuch orders , they fhall require them to appear at the next Court for that Shire : 　 and
alfo fhall certifie the incumbrance found and order by them made , under their hands
unto the faid Court, or appear in perfon to profecute the caufe; where it fhall be heard
and determined for the eafe and conveniencie of Travellers , with due refpect to the
Proprietors coft and damage , but no perfon fhal ftand charged with the repair of common high-wayes through his own ground. [1647]

Idlenes.

*I*T is ordered by this Court and Authoritie therof, that no perfon, Houfholder or
other fhall fpend his time idlely or unproffitably under pain of fuch punifhment
as the Court of Affiftants or County Court fhall think meet to inflict . 　 And for
D 3
this

Conſtabl's care and dutie The power of two Affiſtants	this end it is ordered that the Conſtable of everie place ſhall uſe ſpeciall care and dili-gence to take knowledge of offenders in this kinde , eſpecially of common coaſters, unproffitable fowlers and tobacco takers , and preſent the ſame unto the two next Affiſtants , who ſhall have power to hear and determin the cauſe, or transfer it to the next Court . [1633]

Jefuits.

THIS Court taking into conſideration the great wars , combuſtions and diviſions which are this day in Europe: and that the ſame are obſerved to be rayſed and fo-mented chiefly by the ſecret underminings , and ſolicitations of thoſe of the JeſuiticallOrder, men brought up and devoted to the religion and court of Rome ; which hath occaſioned di-vers States to expell them their territories; for prevention wherof among our ſelves, It is ordered and enacted by Authoritie of this Court ,

One Magiſtr: Bañiſhment.	That no Jeſuit, or ſpiritual or eccleſiaſtical perſon [as they are termed] ordained by the authoritie of the Pope, or Sea of Rome ſhall henceforth at any time repair to, or come within this Juriſdiction : And if any perſon ſhal give juſt cauſe of ſuſpicion that he is one of ſuch Societie or Order he ſhall be brought before ſome of the Magiſtrates, and if he cannot free himſelfe of ſuch ſuſpicion he ſhall be committed to priſon , or bound over to the next Court of Affiſtants , to be tryed and proceeded with by Bañiſh-ment or otherwiſe as the Court ſhall ſee cauſe : and if any perſon ſo baniſhed ſhall be taken the ſecond time within this Juriſdiction upon lawfull tryall and conviction he ſhall be put to death . Provided this Law ſhall not extend to any ſuch Jeſuit, ſpiri-tual or eccleſiaſticall perſon as ſhall be caſt upon our ſhoars, by ſhip-wrack or other ac-cident , ſo as he continue no longer then till he may have opportunitie of paſſage for his departure ; nor to any ſuch as ſhall come in company with any Meſſenger hither upõ publick occaſions , or any Merchant or Maſter of any ſhip,belonging to any place not in emnitie with the State of *England*,or our ſelves, ſo as they depart again with the ſame Meſſenger , Maſter or Merchant , and behave themſelves in-offenſively during their aboad heer . [1647]

Impoſt.

IT is ordered by Authoritie of this Court that *Worronoco* upon *Conecticot* lying within this Juriſdiction ſhall be, and be reputed as a part of the town of *Spring-field* and lyable to all charges there , as other parts of the ſame town , until upon erect-ing ſome other Plantation neer unto it it ſhall be thought fit by this Court to annex it to ſuch new Plantation .

Worronoco. Trading-houſes. Two pence a skin. Forfeit.	It is alſo ordered that the Trading-houſe at *Worronoco* and all other Trading-hou-ſes erected or to be erected , mainteined or uſed within this Juriſdi&ion , for trading with the Indians only or chiefly ſhall be contributarie to all publick and common char-ges,both in Town and Countrie , and everie ſuch perſon as ſhall inhabit or trade in any ſuch Trading-houſe or neer the ſame ſhall pay unto the publick Treaſurie (by the hands of ſuch as ſhall be aſſigned to receive the ſame) for everie skin of Beaver,Otter, Bear or Mooſe two pence . And if ſuch perſon ſo aſſigned ſhall have cauſe to ſuſpect that any ſuch Trader hath not given a true account of all ſuch skins ſo traded , he ſhall inform one of the next Magiſtrates therof , who ſhall ſend for ſuch Trader and require him to deliver account upon his oath , which if he ſhall refuſe to doe , he may commit him to priſon or take *Bond* with Suretie for his appearance at the next Court of Affiſtants to an-ſwer his contempt, and be proceeded with according to juſtice . And it is farther ordered that all ſuch skins ſo received, by way of trading , in, or neer any ſuch Trading-houſe for which the ſaid *Impoſt* of two pence a skin ſhall not be ſatisfied within one week after demaund therof ſhall be forfeited to the publick Treaſurie , or the value therof; to be levied by *Warrant* from any one Magiſtrate upon any skins or other goods in ſuch Trading-houſe . [1647]

2 *For the better fupport of the Government of this Common-wealth and the maintain-*
ance of Fortificatious for the protecting and fafe-guarding of our Coafts and Harbours, for
our felves and others that come to trade with us, it is ordered by this Court and the Au-
thoritie therof,

That every perfon, Merchant, Seaman, or other that fhall bring wines into any
our Harbours, in any fhips or veffels whatfoever (except they come directly from *Eng-*
land as their firft Port) before they land any of the faid wines, more or leffe, fhall firft
make entrie of as many Buts, Pipes, or other veffels, as they or any of them fhall put on
fhore, by a note under their hands, delivered unto the Officer at his houfe (who is to receive the Cuftoms) upon pain of forfeiture and confifcation of all fuch wines as are landed before fuch entrie made, wherefoever found, the one halfe to the Countrie, the other
halfe to the Officer: and the Merchants or Owners of fuch wines of any kinde, as foon
as he lands them, fhall deliver and pay unto the faid Officer, what is due for Cuftom of
them according to this Order, in wine according to the proportion of the goodnes of the
parcel that is brought in, as the Officer and Owner can agree, to the contentment and fatisfaction of the faid Officer, or elfe the Owner and Officer to nominate a third man
who fhall put a finall price between them, in point of valuation of the wines for Cuftoms: but if they cannot agree, upon notice from the Officer unto the Treafurer for the
time being, he fhall determin the price therof, and being fo ordered the Officer and
Merchant fhall accept therof.

And it is farther ordered that he that is the cheife Officer to receive fuch Cuftomes fhall
have under him a Deputie or Deputies who fhall be as Searchers or waytors in feverall
places to take up fuch wines, by the cheif Officers appointment, and to take notice of
what is landed in any place that the Country be not defrauded, who fhall have fuch due
recompence as the cheif Officer in his difcretion fhall agree with them for, either by the
Butt or Pipe or by the year. All wines to pay cuftoms according to thefe rates following *viz:* for every Butt or pipe of *Fyall* wines or any other wines of thofe Weftern If-
lands five fhillings. For everie Pipe of *Madarie* wines fix fhillings eight pence. For
everie Butt or Pipe of *Sherris* fack, *Malego* or *Canarie* wines ten fhillings. For *Mufca-*
dels, *Malmfies* and other wines from the *Streights* ten fhillings. For Baftards, Tents &
Alligants ten fhillings: and proportionably for greater or leffer veffels of each kinde.
For everie Hogfhead of French wines two fhillings fix pence, and proportionably for
greater or leffer veffels.

And for better recovering of any fuch Cuftoms of wines or forfeitures, for not enter-
ing according to this Order and for refufing of payment of fuch Cuftoms to the fatisfaction
of the Officer, it is farther ordered,

That the faid Officer hath heerby power and is required to goe into all Houfes or
Cellars where he knoweth or fufpecteth any wine to be, and from time to time fhall feiz
upon fuch wines as are not entred according to this Order: and alfo feiz upon, and
take poffeffion of fo much wines as to make payment of what Cuftom is due according
to entries made, and is refufed or neglected to be paid in due manner according to this
Order. And all Conftables and other Officers are heerby required to affift and ayd
the Officer in the difcharge of his duty, and helping to break open fuch Houfes or Cellars, if the Owners of fuch wines fhal refufe to open their doors or deliver their keys in a
peacable way. And any Smith, Carter, Owner of boat, Porter or other that fhall be
required by the Officer to put to their hand to help and affift in taking, loading & tranf-
porting fuch wines for the ufe of the Country, and fhall refufe or neglect fuch fervice for
due hire fhall forfeit to the common Treafurie ten fhillings for everie fuch default, to be
levied by the Conftable by *warrant* from any one Magiftrate. And all debts due unto
the Countrie for cuftom of wines, where wines are not to be found, they are to be reco-
vered by way of Action, according to a courfe of law as in other cafes, and this Order
to be in force to recover Cuftoms from all thofe that have landed wine in this Jurifdiction already and not payd Cuftom.

Margin notes:
- Entrie of wine
- on payn of forfeiture.
- Cuftom when payd.
- Cuftomers Deputie.
- Rates of wine
- Cuftomers power.
- Conft: &c: to ayd the Cuftomer:
- on penalty of 10 fs.
- Cuftom reco-vered by Actio

Impreſſes.

Only by Gen
Court upõ due
recompence.

I T is ordered, and by this Court declared, that no man ſhall be compelled to any publick work, or ſervice, unleſſe the Preſſe be grounded upon ſome act of the General Court; and have reaſonable allowance therfore: nor ſhall any man be compel-

Pref-free, for
defects:

led in perſon to any office, work, wars, or other publick ſervice that is neceſſarily and ſufficiently exempted, by any natural or perſonal impediment ; as by want of years, greatnes of age, defect of minde, failing of ſenſes, or impotencye of lims . Nor ſhall

from forrein
warrs:

any man be compelled to go out of this Juriſdiction upon any offenſive wars, which this Common-wealth, or any of our freinds or confœderates ſhall voluntarily undertake; but only upõ ſuch vindictive and defenſive wars, in our own behalf, or the behalf of our

Limitation.

freinds and confœderates; as ſhall be enterprized by the counſell, and conſent of a General Court, or by Authoritie derived from the ſame . Nor ſhall any mans cattle or

for cattle and
goods.
Limitation
twofold.

goods of what kinde ſoever be preſſed, or taken for any publick uſe or ſervice; unles it be by *Warrant* grounded upon ſome act of the General Court : nor without ſuch reaſonable prizes and hire as the ordinarie rates of the Countrie doe afford . And if his cattle or goods ſhall periſh, or ſuffer damage in ſuch ſervice, the Owner ſhall be ſuffici-

Recompence

ently recompenced. [1641]

Impriſonment.

Who be bayl-
able.

I T is ordered, and by this Court declared; that no mans perſon ſhall be reſtreined or impriſoned by any authoritie whatſoever before the Law hath ſentenced him therto: if he can put in ſufficient ſecuritie, *Bayle* or *Mainprize* for his appearance, and good behaviour in the mean time: unles it be in crimes Capital, and contempt in open Court, and in ſuch caſes where ſome expreſſe Act of Court doth allow it. [1641]

Jndians.

Licence to
buy their land.

I T is ordered by Authoritie of this Court ; that no perſon whatſoever ſhall henceforth buy land of any Indian, without licence firſt had & obtained of the General Court: and if any ſhall offend heerin, ſuch land ſo bought ſhall be forfeited to the Countrie .

none muſt re-
pair their guns

Nor ſhall any man within this Juriſdiction directly or indirectly amend, repair, or cauſe to be amended or repaired any gun, ſmall or great, belonging to any Indian,

nor ſell gun
or amunition
on pen: of
10 li.

nor ſhall indeavour the ſame . Nor ſhall ſell or give to any Indian, directly or indirectly anyſuch gun, or any gun-powder, ſhot or lead, or ſhot-mould, or any militarie weapons or armour: upon payn of ten pounds fine, at the leaſt for everie ſuch offence: and that the court of Aſſiſtants ſhall have power to increaſe the Fine; or to impoſe corporall puniſhment (where a Fine cannot be had) at their diſcretion .

Who may re-
ſtrein them frõ
profaning the
Sabbath.

It is alſo ordered by the Authoritie aforeſaid that everie town ſhall have power to reſtrein all Indians from profaning the Lords day. [1633 1637 1641]

2 *Wheras it appeareth to this Court that notwithſtanding the former Laws, made a-gainſt ſelling of guns, powder and Amunition to the Indians, they are yet ſupplyed by indirect means, it is therfore ordered by this Court and Authoritie therof* ;

No arms ſold
to Indian or
Forreiner \without licence.

That if any perſon after publication heerof, ſhall ſell, give or barter any gun or guns, powder, bullets, ſhot or lead to any Indian whatſoever, or unto any perſon inhabiting out of this Juriſdiction without licence of this Court, or the court of Aſſiſtants, or ſome two Magiſtrates, he ſhall forfeit for everie gun ſo ſold, given or bar-

on forf: for a
gun 10 li,
for 1 li. powder 5 li.
1 li. ſhot &c:
40 ſs.

tered ten pounds: and for everie pound of powder five pounds: and for everie pound of bullets, ſhot or lead fourty ſhillings: and ſo proportionably for any greater or leſſer quantitie . [1642]

3 It is ordered by this Court and Authoritie therof, that in all places, the Engliſh and ſuch others as co-inhabit within our Juriſdiction ſhall keep their cattle frõ deſtroy-

preſervation of
their corn.

ing the Indians corn, in any ground where they have right to plant; and if any of their corn be deſtroyed for want of fencing, or hearding; the town ſhall make ſatiſfaction, and ſhall have power among themſelves to lay the charge where the occaſion of the damage did ariſe . Provided that the Indians ſhall make proof that the cattle of ſuch a town, farm, or perſon did the damage . And for encouragement of of the Indians toward the fencing in of their corn fields , such towns, farms or persons, whose cattle may annoy them that way , shall direct, assist and help them in felling of trees, ryving, and sharpening of rayls, & holing of posts : allowing one English-man to three or more Indians . And shall also draw the fencing into place for them, and allow one man a day or two toward the setting up the same, and either lend or sell them tools to finish it . Provided that such Indians, to whom the Countrie, or any town hath given, or shall give ground to plant upon, or that shall purchase ground of the English shall fence such their corn fields or ground at their own charge as the English doe or should doe ; and if any Indians refuse to fence their corn ground (being tendred help as aforesaid) in the presence and hearing of any Magistrate or selected Townsmen being met together they shall keep off all cattle or lose one half of their damages .

> *Help in Fencing.*

And it is also ordered that if any harm be done at any time by the Indians unto the English in their cattle; the Governour or Deputie Governour with two of the Assistants or any three Magistrates or any County Court may order satisfaction according to law and justice . [1640 1648]

> *Indians hurting cattle Satisfaction.*

4 *Considering that one end in planting these parts was to propagate the true Religion unto the Indians : and that divers of them are become subjects to the English and have ingaged themselves to be willing and ready to understand the Law of God , it is therfore ordered and decreed,*

That such necessary and wholsom Laws, which are in force, and may be made from time to time , to reduce them to civilitie of life shall be once in the year (if the times be safe) made known to them, by such fit persons as the General Court shall nominate , having the help of some able Interpreter with them .

Considering also that interpretation of tongues is appointed of God for propagating the Truth: and may therfore have a blessed successe in the hearts of others in due season, it is therfore farther ordered and decreed ,

That two Ministers shall be chosen by the Elders of the Churches everie year at the Court of Election, and so be sent with the consent of their Churches (with whomsoever will freely offer themselves to accompany them in that service) to make known the heavenly counsell of God among the Indians in most familiar manner , by the help of some able Interpreter ; as may be most available to bring them unto the knowledge of the truth , and their conversation to the Rules of Jesus Christ . And for that end that somthing be allowed them by the General Court, to give away freely unto those Indians whom they shall perceive most willing & ready to be instructed by them.

> *Means for their instruction in Religion*

And it is farther ordered and decreed by this Court; that no Indian shall at any time *powaw* , or performe outward worship to their false gods: or to the devil in any part of our Jurisdiction ; whether they be such as shall dwell heer, or shall come hither : and if any shall transgresse this Law, the *Powawer* shall pay five pounds; the Procurer five pounds; and every other countenancing by his presence or otherwise being of age of discretion twenty shillings . [1646]

> *Against their false worship.*

Inditements .

IF any person shall be indicted of any capital crime (who is not then in *durance*) & shall refuse to render his person to some Magistrate within one month after three Proclaimations publickly made in the town where he usually abides , there being a month betwixt Proclaimation and Proclaimation , his lands and goods shall be seized to the use of the common Treasurie , till he make his lawfull appearance . And such withdrawing of himselfe shall stand in stead of one wittnes to prove his crime , unles he can make it appear to the Court that he was necessarily hindred. [1646]

In-keepers, Tippling, Drunkenes.

FORASMUCH *as there is a necessary use of houses of common entertainment in every Common-wealth , and of such as retail wine, beer and victuals; yet because there are so many abuses of that lawfull libertie , both by persons entertaining and persons entertained , there is also need of strict Laws and Rules to regulate such an employment: It is therfore ordered by this Court and Authoritie therof ;*

E   That

That no perfon or perfons fhall at any time under any pretence or colour whatfoever undertake to be a common Victuailer, Keeper of a Cooks fhop, or houfe for common entertainment , Taverner, or publick feller of wine, ale, beer or ftrong-water (by re-tale), nor fhall any fell wine privatly in his houfe or out of doors by a leffe quantitie, or under a quarter cask : without approbation of the felected Townf-men and Licence of the Shire Court where they dwell: upon pain of forfeiture of five pounds for everie fuch offence, or imprifonment at pleafure of the Court, where fatis-faction cannot be had.

And every perfon fo licenced for common entertainment fhall have fome inoffen-five Signe obvious for ftrangers direction , and fuch as have no fuch Signe after three months fo licenced from time to time fhall lofe their licence : and others allowed in their ftead . And any licenced perfon that felleth beer fhall not fell any above two-pence the ale-quart: upon penaltie of three fhillings four pence for everie fuch offence. And it is permitted to any that will to fell beer out of doors at a pennie the ale-quart and under .

Neither fhall any fuch licenced perfon aforefaid fuffer any to be drunken, or drink exceffively *viz:* above half a pinte of wine for one perfon at one time; or to con-tinue tippling above the fpace of half an hour , or at unfeafonable times, or after nine of the clock at night in, or about any of their houfes on penaltie of five fhillings for everie fuch offence .

And everie perfon found drunken *viz:* fo that he be therby bereaved or difabled in the ufe of his underftanding, appearing in his fpeech or gefture in any the faid houf-es or elfewhere fhall forfeit ten fhillings . And for exceffive drinking three fhillings four pence . And for continuing above half an hour tippling two fhillings fix pence. And for tippling at unfeafonable times , or after nine a clock at night five fhillings: for everie offence in thefe particulars being lawfully convict therof . And for want of payment fuch fhall be imprifoned untill they pay: or be fet in the *Stocks* one hour or more [in fome open place] as the weather will permit not exceeding three hours at one time .

Provided notwithftanding fuch licenced perfons may entertain fea-faring men, or land travellers in the night-feafon , when they come firft on fhore, or from their journy for their neceffarie refrefhment, or when they prepare for their voyage or jour-nie the next day early; fo there be no diforder among them; and alfo Strangers, Lodg-ers or other perfons in an orderly way may continue in fuch houfes of common enter-tainment during meal times, or upon lawfull bufines what time their occafions fhall require .

Nor fhall any Merchant, Cooper, Owner or Keeper of wines or other perfons that have the government of them fuffer any perfon to drink to exceffe, or drunkenes, in any their wine-Cellars, Ships, or other veffels or places where wines doe lye; on pain to forfeit for each perfon fo doing ten fhillings .

And if any perfon offend in drunkenes, exceffive or long drinking the fecõd time they fhall pay double Fines . And if they fall into the fame offence the third time they fhall pay treble Fines . And if the parties be not able to pay the Fines then he that is found drunk fhall be punifhed by whipping to the number of ten ftripes: and he that offends in exceffive or long drinking fhall be put into the ftocks for three hours when the weather may not hazzard his life or lims . And if they offend the fourth time they fhall be imprifoned untill they put in two fufficient Sureties for their good behaviour .

And it is farther ordered that if any perfon that keepeth, or heerafter fhall keep a common houfe of entertainmen , fhall be lawfully convicted the third time for any offence againft this Law: he fhall (for the fpace of three years next enfuing the faid conviction) be difabled to keep any fuch houfe of entertainment , or fell wine, beer or the like ; unles the Court aforefaid fhall fee caufe to continue them.

It is farther ordered that everie In-keeper , or Victuailer fhall provide for the
entertainment

Marginal notes:

No common Victuailer. Cook, Vintner &c· without licence.

On pen: 5 li.

Signe

No beer above two pence the quart
Any may fel out of doors of 1 d. a quart.

In-holders forfeit

Penalty of drũknes 10 fs. exc: 3 fs. 4 d. Tipl: unfea-fonably.

Stocks.

Provifo,

The laws fur-ther extent

Secõd offence double penal: Third offen: Whipping,

ftocks.

Fourth offen:

Victuailer cõvict: a third time difabled:

of ftrangers horfes *viz:* one or more inclofures for Summer and hay and provender for Winter with convenient ftable room and attendance under penaltie of two fhillings fix pence for everie dayes default , and double damage to the partie therby wronged (except it be by inevitable accident. | Provifiõ for horfes.

And it is farther ordered by the Authoritie aforefaid, that no Taverner or feller of wine by retale, licenced as aforefaid fhall take above nine pounds profit by the Butt or Pipe of wine, (and proportionably for all other veffels) toward his waft in drawing and otherwife: out of which allowance everie fuch Taverner or Vintner fhall pay fifty fhillings by the Butt or Pipe and proportionably for all other veffels to the Countrie. For which he fhall account with the Auditor general or his Deputie every fix months and difcharge the fame . All which they may doe by felling fix pence a quart in retale (which they fhall no time exceed) more then it coft by the Butt, befide the benefit of their art and myfterie which they know how to make ufe of . And everie Taverner or Vintner fhall give a true account and notice unto the Auditor or his Deputie of everie veffell of wine he buies from time to time within three dayes ; upon pain of forfeiting the fame or the value therof . | Vintner. / pay 50 fs. y̆ Butt ro the Countrie. / give account.

And all fuch as retale ftrong waters fhall pay in like manner two pence upon everie quart to the ufe of the Country, who alfo fhall give notice to the Auditor or his Deputie of everie cafe and bottle or other quantitie they buy within three dayes upon payn of forfeiture as before . | Two pence a quart for retail of ftrong water.

Alfo it is ordered that in all places where week day Lectures are kept, all Taverners, Victuailers and Tablers that are within a mile of the Meeting-houfe, fhall from time to time clear their houfes of all perfons able to goe to the Meeting, during the time of the exercife (except upon extraordinary caufe, for the neceffarie refrefhing of ftrangers ũexpectedly repairing to them) upõ pain of five fhillings for every fuch offence over and befides the penalties incurred by this Law for any other diforder . | Com: houfes cleared in Lecture time.

It is alfo ordered that all offences againft this Law may be heard and determined by any one Magiftrate, who fhall heerby have power by *Warrant* to fend for parties, and witneffes, and to examin the faid witneffes upon oath and the parties without oath, concerning any of thefe offences: and upon due conviction either by view of the faid Magiftrate, or affirmation of the Conftable, and one fufficient witnes with circumftances concurring, or two witneffes, or confeffion of the partie to levie the faid feverall fines, by *Warrant* to the Conftable for that end, who fhall be accountable to the Auditor for the fame . | One Magiftr: may hear &c. / Fines levied.

And if any perfon fhall voluntarily confeffe his offence againft this Law in any the particulars therof, his oath fhall be taken in evidence and ftand good againft any other offending at the fame time. | Delinquents teftimonie.

Laftly, it is ordered by the Authoritie aforefaid that all Conftables may, and fhall from time to time duly make fearch throughout the limits of their towns upon Lords dayes, and Lecture dayes, in times of Exercife; and alfo at all other times, fo oft as they fhall fee caufe for all offences and offenders againft this Law in any the pariculars therof . And if upon due information, or complaint of any of their Inhabitants , or other credible perfons whether Taverner, Victuailer, Tabler or other ; they fhall refufe or neglect to make fearch as aforefaid , or fhall not to their power perform all other things belonging to their place and Office of Conftablefhip : then upon complaint and due proof before any one Magiftrate within three months after fuch refufall or neglect; they fhall be fined for everie fuch offence ten fhillings , to be levied by the Marfhal as in other cafes by *Warrant* from fuch Magiftrate before whom they are convicted, or *Warrant* from the Treafurer upon notice from fuch Magiftrate . [1645 1646 1647] *See Gaming, Licences.* | Conft: fearch / Conftables neglect.

Iuries , Iurors.

I T is ordered by this Court and Authoritie therof , that the Conftable of everie town upon *Proces* from the Recorder of each Court , fhall give timely notice to the Freemen of their town, to choof fo many able difcreet men as the *Proces* fhal direct

E 2   which

Juries for tryals.

which men ſo choſen he ſhall warn to attend the Court whereto they are appointed, and ſhall make return of the *Proces* unto the Recorder aforeſaid: which men ſo cho-ſen ſhall be *impannelled* and ſworn truly to try betwixt partie and partie, who ſhall

Verdict according to fact

finde the matter of fact with the damages and coſts according to their evidence, and the Judges ſhall declare the Sentence (or direct the Jurie to finde) according to the law.

Equitie and law in the ſame caſe

And if there be any matter of apparent equitie as upon the forfeiture of an Obligation, breach of covenant without damage, or the like, the Bench ſhall determin ſuch matter of equitie .

Tryall for life &c: by 12 m̄

2 Nor ſhall any tryall paſſe upon any for life or banniſhment but by a ſpecial Jurie ſo ſummoned for that purpoſe , or by the General Court.

Juries for inquirie

3 It is alſo ordered by the Authoritie aforeſaid that there ſhall be Grand-Juries ſum-moned everie year unto the ſeveral Courts, in each Jurisdiction; to inform the Court of any miſdemeanours that they ſhall know or hear to be committed by any perſon or

may be for tryal alſo,

perſons whatſoever within this Juriſdiction . And to doe any other ſervice of the Common-wealth that according to law they ſhall be injoyned to by the ſaid Court;

Poſitive verd: Non liquet

and in all caſes wherin evidence is ſo obſcure or defective that the Jurie cannot clearly and ſafely give a poſitive verdict, whether it be Grand, or Petty Jurie, it ſhall have libertie to give a *Non liquet* or a ſpecial verdict, in which laſt, that is, a ſpecial verdict

Partial verd:

the judgement of the Cauſe ſhall be left unto the Bench . And all Jurors ſhall have libertie in matters of fact if they cannot finde the *main iſſue* yet to finde and preſent in their verdict ſo much as they can.

Differ: twixt Jury & Bench iſſued

4 And if the Bench and Jurors ſhall ſo differ at any time about their verdict that either of them cannot proceed with peace of conſcience , the Caſe ſhall be referred to the General Court who ſhall take the queſtion from both and determin it.

Jurie in their doubts may adviſe opēly none ſerv but once a year except:

5 And it is farther ordered that whenſoever any Jurie of tryalls , or Jurors are not clear in their judgements or conſciences , concerning any Caſe wherin they are to give their verdict , they ſhall have libertie, in open Court to adviſe with any man they ſhall think fit to reſolve or direct them, before they give in their verdict . And no Free-man ſhall be compelled to ſerve upon Juries above one ordinary Court in a year : ex-cept Grand-jurie men, who ſhall hold two Courts together at the leaſt, and ſuch others as ſhall be ſummoned to ſerve in caſe of life and death or banniſhment. [1634] [1641 1642] *See Secreſie.*

Iuſtice.

Forreiners libertie.

I T is ordered, and by this Court declared; that every perſon within this Juris-diction, whether Inhabitant or other ſhall enjoy the ſame juſtice and law that is general for this Juriſdiction which wee conſtitute and execute one towards another, in all caſes proper to our cogniſance without partialitie or delay . [1641]

Lands , Free lands.

I T is ordered, and by this Court declared ; that all our Lands and Heritages ſhall be free from all *Fines* and *Licences* upon alienations, and from all *Hariots*, *Ward-ſhips*, *Liveries*, *Primerſeizins*, year, day and waſt , *Eſcheats* and forfeitures , upon the death of Parents or Anceſters, be they natural, unnatural, caſual or judicial and that for ever. [1641] *See Abilitie, Eſcheats, Strangers.*

Leather.

T HIS Court taking into ſerious conſideration the ſeveral deceits and abuſes which in other places have been and are commonly practiced by the *Tanners, Curriers* and workers of leather, as alſo the abnſes and inconveniences which acrue to the ſeverall mem-bers of this Common-wealth, by leather not ſufficiently tanned and wrought , which is oc-caſioned by the negligence and unskilfullnes of thoſe ſeverall tradeſ-men which before, in, & after it is in the hands of the Tanner may be much bettered or impaired , for preven-tion wherof, it is ordered by this Court and the Authoritie therof;

That no perſon uſing or occupying the feat or myſterie of a Butcher, Currier, or
ſhoe-maker

Shoe-maker by himfelfe or any other , fhall ufe or exercife the feat or myfterie of a Tanner on pain of forfeiture of fix fhillings eight pence for everie hyde or skin by him or them fo tanned whileft he or they fhall ufe or occupie any of the myfteries aforefaid . *Butcher Cur rier Shoem: no Tanner.*

Nor fhall any Tanner during his ufing the faid trade of tanning , ufe or occupie the feat or myfterie of either Butcher , Currier or Shoo-maker by himfelf or any other upon pain of the like forfeiture . *Tanner no Butcher, Cur rier Shoom.*

Nor fhall any Butcher by himfelf or any other perfon gafh or cut any hyde of ox, bull, fteer, or cow in fleaing therof, or otherwife wherby the fame fhall be impaired or hurt , on pain of forfeiture for everie fuch gafh or cut in any hyde or skin twelve pence . *Gafh : hyde or skin 12 d*

Nor fhall any perfon or perfons henceforth bargain, buy , make any contract, or befpeak any rough hyde of ox, bull, fteer or cow in the hair , but only fuch perfons as have and doe ufe and exercife the art of tanning . *Rough hyds*

Nor fhall any perfon or perfons ufing , or which fhall ufe the myfterie or facultie of tanning at any time or times heerafter , offer or put to fale any kinde of leather, which fhall be infufficiently or not throughly tanned , or which fhall not then have been after the tanning therof well and throughly dryed , upon pain of forfeiting fo much of his or their faid leather as by any Searcher or Sealer of leather lawfully ap-pointed fhall be found infufficiently tanned , or not throughly dryed as aforefaid. *well tañed & dryed. Penaltie.*

Nor fhall any perfon or perfons ufing or occupying the myfterie of tanning, fet any their Fats in tan-hills or other places , where the woozes or leather put to tan in the fame fhall or may take any unkinde heats ; nor fhall put any leather into any hot or warm woozes whatfoever on pain of twenty pounds for everie fuch offence . *Leather tak- ing ũkinde heats. Penaltie 20 li*

Nor fhall any perfon or perfons ufing or occupying the myfterie or facultie of currying , currie any kinde of leather , except it be well and throughly tanned ; nor fhall currie any hyde being not throughly dryed after his wet feafon ; in which wet feafon he fhall not ufe any ftale , urin , or any other deceitfull or fubtil mixture , thing, way or means to corrupt or hurt the fame : nor fhall currie any leather meet for utter fole leather with any other then good hard tallow , nor with any leffe of that then the leather will receive : nor fhall currie any kinde of leather meet for upper leather and inner foles, but with good and fufficient ftuffe, being frefh and not falt, and throughly liquored till it will receive no more : nor fhall burn or fcald any hyde or leather in the currying , but fhall work the fame fufficiently in all points and refpects; on pain of forfeiture for everie fuch offence or act done contrary to the true meaning of this Order the full value of everie fuch hyde marred by his evil workmanfhip or handling , which fhall be judged by two , or more fufficient and honeft skilfull perfons , Curriers or others , on their oath given to them for that end by any Affiftant . *Curriers duty* *Penaltie.*

And everie town where need is,or fhall be, fhall choofe one or two perfons of the moft honeft and skilfull within their feveral Townfhips, and prefent them unto the County Court, or one Magiftrate who fhall appoint and fwear the faid perfons: by their difcretion to make fearch and view within the Precincts of their limits as oft as they fhall think good and need fhall be , who fhall have a Mark or Seal prepared by each town for that purpofe , and the faid Searchers or one of them fhall keep the fame, and therewith fhall feal fuch leather as they fhall finde fufficient in all points and no other . *Searchers fworn. their dutie* *to feale.*

And if the faid Searchers , or any of them fhall finde any leather fold, or offered to be fold , brought , or offered to be fearched or fealed , which fhall be tanned, wrought, converted or ufed contrary to the true intent and meaning of this Order, it fhall be lawfull for the faid Searchers , or any of them to feiz all fuch leather and to retain the fame in their cuftodie , untill fuch time as it be tryed by fuch Tryers, *feiz defective*

E 3   and

Tryers of lea-ther feized

and in fuch manner as in this Order is appointed *viz:* upon the forfeiture of any leather the Officer fo feizing the fame , fhall within three dayes call to him four or fix men, honeft, and skilfull in fuch ware to view the fame in the prefence of the partie (who fhal have timely notice therof) or without him, who fhall certifie upon their oaths unto the next County Court for that Shire , or unto one of the Affiftants the defect of the fame leather , except the partie fhall before fubmit to their judgement .

Searching wares made of leather. Searcher defaulting.

The like power fhall the faid Searcher have to fearch all leather wrought into fhoos and boots , as alfo to feize all fuch as they finde to be made of infufficient lea-ther , or not well and fufficiently wrought up . And if any Searcher or Sealer of leather fhall refufe with convenient fpeed to feal any leather fufficiently tanned , wrought and ufed according to the true meaning of this Order , or fhall feal that which fhall be infufficient , then everie fuch Searcher and Sealer of leather fhall forfeit for everie fuch offence the full value of fo much as fhall be infufficiently tanned .

Searchers Fee

payd by the Tanner

And the Fees for fearching and fealing of leather fhall be one pennie a hyde for any parcel leffe then five , and for all other parcels after the rate of fix pence a *Dekar* ; which the Tanner fhall pay upon the fealing of the faid leather from time to time .

Fines diftr:

Laftly , it is ordered by the Authoritie aforefaid that the feverall Fines and For-feitures in this Order mentioned , fhall be equally divided into three parts and diftri-buted as followeth *viz:* one part to the common Treafurie of the Shire wherin the offence is committed , another third part to the common Treafurie of the Townfhip where fuch offender inhabiteth , and the other third part to the Seizer or Seizers of fuch leather , fhoos or boots, as is infufficiently tanned, curried or wrought from time to time . [1642]

Levies .

FORASMVCH as the *Marfhals* and other *Officers* have complained to this Court that they are oftentimes in great doubt how to demean themfelves in the execution of their offices , it is ordered by the Authoritie of this Court ;

Officer fhall demaund upō refufal may break open &c

That in cafe of Fines and Affeffements to be levied, and upon Execution in civil Actions,the Officer fhall demand the fame of the partie, or at his houfe or place of ufuall abode , and upon refufall or non-payment he fhall have power (calling the Conftable if he fee caufe for his affiftance) to break open the door of any houfe, cheft , or place where he fhall have notice that any goods lyable to fuch Levie or

the perfon

Execution fhall be ; and if he be to take the perfon he may doe the like , if upon demand he fhall refufe to render himfelf .

Neceffarie charge

And whatever charges the Officer fhall neceffarily be put unto upon any fuch occafion , he fhall have power to levie the fame , as he doth the debt , Fine, or Exe-cution : and where the Officer fhall levie any fuch goods upon execution as cannot be conveyed to the place where the partie dwells , for whom fuch Execution fhall be levied, without confiderable charge , he fhall levie the faid charge alfo with the Execution .

Fines Things not fubject to levie. Officer not bound to look out eftate

The like order fhall be obferved in levying of Fines . Provided it fhall not be lawfull for fuch Officer to levie any mans neceffarie bedding, apparel, tools, or Arms, neither implements of houfhold which are for the neceffarie upholding of his life, but in fuch cafes he fhall levie his land or perfon according to law : and in no cafe fhall the Officer be put to feek out any mans eftate farther then his place of a-bode ; but if the partie will not difcover his goods or lands , the Officer may take his perfon .

And it is alfo ordered and declared that if any Officer fhall doe injurie to any by colour of his Office , in thefe or any other cafes he fhall be lyable upon com-plaint of the partie wronged , by Action or Information to make full reftitution. [1647]

Liberties com-

Liberties Common.

IT is ordered by this Court , decreed and declared ; that everie man whether Inhabitant or Forreiner, Free or not Free ſhall have libertie to come to any pub-lick Court, Counſell, or Town-meeting ; and either by ſpeech or writing, to move any lawfull, ſeaſonable, or material queſtion;   or to preſent any neceſſarie motion, complaint, petition, bill or information wherof that Meeting hath proper cogniſance, ſo it be done in convenient time, due order and reſpeċtive manner. [1641] *(Freedom in publ. Aſſemb. [Freemen For[nõ-Frem. [Strangers.)*

2 Everie Inhabitant who is an houſ-holder ſhall have free fiſhing and fowling, in any great Ponds, Bayes, Coves and Rivers ſo far as the Sea ebs and flows, within the precinċts of the town where they dwell, unles the Free-men of the ſame town, or the General Court have otherwiſe appropriated them .   Provided that no town ſhall appropriate to any particular perſon or perſons, any great Pond conteining more then ten acres of land: and that no man ſhall come upon anothers proprietie without their leave otherwiſe then as heerafter expreſſed ; the which clearly to determin, it is de-clared that in all creeks, coves and other places, about and upon ſalt water where the Sea ebs and flows ,   the Proprietor of the land adjoyning ſhall have proprietie to the low water mark where the Sea doth not ebb above a hundred rods, and not more whereſoever it ebs farther .   Provided that ſuch Proprietor ſhall not by this libertie have power to ſtop or hinder the paſſage of boats or other veſſels in, or through any ſea creeks, or coves to other mens houſes or lands .   And for great Ponds lying in com-mon though within the bounds of ſome town, it ſhall be free for any man to fiſh and fowl there, and may paſſe and repaſſe on foot through any mans proprietie for that end, ſo they treſpaſſe not upon any mans corn or meadow . [1641 1647] *(Fiſhing and fowl: where the Sea ebbs and flows except pro-prieties. — to low water not exceeding 100 rod. — water paſſag: free & ponds above 10 acrs)*

3 Every man of, or within this Juriſdiċtion ſhall have free libertie, (notwithſtand-ing any civil power) to remove both himſelf and his familie at their pleaſure out of the ſame .   Provided there be no legal impediment to the contrary . [1641] *See Arreſts, Records, Witneſſes.* *(Removals free)*

Lying.

WHERAS *truth in words as well as in aċtions is required of all men, eſpecially of Chiſtians who are the profeſſed Servants of the God of Truth ;   and wheras all lying is contrary to truth, and ſome ſorts of lyes are not only ſinfull (as all lyes are) but alſo pernicious to the Publick-weal, and injurious to particular perſons ; it is therfore order-ed by this Court and Authoriti'e therof,*

That everie perſon of the age of diſcretion [which is accounted fourteen years] who ſhall wittingly and willingly make, or publiſh any Lye which may be pernicious to the publick weal , or tending to the damage or injurie of any particular perſon, or with intent to deceive and abuſe the people with falſe news or reports :   and the ſame duly proved in any Court or before any one Magiſtrate (who hath heerby power graunted to hear, and determin all offences againſt this Law) ſuch perſon ſhall be fined for the firſt offence ten ſhillings, or if the partie be unable to pay the ſame then to be ſet in the *ſtocks* ſo long as the ſaid Court or Magiſtrate ſhall appoint , in ſome open place, not exceeding two hours .   For the ſecond offence in that kinde wherof any ſhall be legally conviċted the ſum of twenty ſhillings , or be whipped upon the naked body not exceeding ten ſtripes .   And for the third offence that way fourty ſhillings, or if the partie be unable to pay , then to be whipped with more ſtripes, not exceeding fifteen .   And if yet any ſhall offend in like kinde, and be legally conviċted therof, ſuch perſon, male or female, ſhall be fined ten ſhillings a time more then formerly: or if the partie ſo offending be unable to pay , then to be whipped with five, or ſix more ſtripes then formerly not exceeding fourty at any time . *(Age of diſ-cretiõ 14 years — One Magiſtr. may hear &c: Firſt offence 10 ſs or ſtocks. — Sec: offence 20 ſhill: or whipped. Third offence 40 ſhill: or whipped, Fourth offen: 10 ſs more or 5 ſtripes more)*

The aforeſaid fines ſhall be levied, or ſtripes infliċted either by the Marſhal of that Juriſdiċtion , or Conſtable of the Town where the offence is committed according *(Who ſhall excecute.)*

according as the Court or Magiſtrate ſhall direct . And ſuch fines ſo levied ſhall be paid to the Treaſurie of that Shire where the Cauſe is tried .

Libertie to appeal.

And if any perſon ſhall finde himſelfe greived with the ſentence of any ſuch Magiſtrate out of Court, he may appeal to the next Court of the ſame Shire, giving ſufficient ſecuritie to proſecute his appeal and abide the Order of the Court . And if the ſaid Court ſhall judge his appeal cauſleſſe, he ſhall be double fined and pay the charges of the Court during his Action , or corrected by whipping as aforeſaid not exceeding fourtie ſtripes; and pay the coſts of Court and partie complaining or informing , and of Wittneſſes in the Caſe .

under 14 years corrected by Parents. the parties Action ſaved

And for all ſuch as being under age of diſcretion that ſhall offend in lying contrary to this Order their Parents or Maſters ſhall give them due correction , and that in the preſence of ſome Officer if any Magiſtrate ſhall ſo appoint . Provided alſo that no perſon ſhall be barred of his juſt Action of Slaunder, or otherwiſe by any proceeding upon this Order. [1645]

Magiſtrates.

*T*HIS Court being ſenſible of the great diſorder growing in this Common-wealth through the contempts caſt upon the civil Authoritie, which willing to prevent, doe order and decree;

Defame &c:

That whoſoever ſhal henceforth openly or willingly defame any Court of juſtice, or the Sentences or proceedings of the ſame, or any of the Magiſtrates or other Judges of any ſuch Court in reſpect of any Act or Sentence therin paſſed , and being therof

Convict: Penaltie.

lawfully convict' in any General Court or Court of Aſſiſtants ſhall be puniſhed for the ſame by Fine, Impriſonment, *Disfranchiſement* or Banniſhment as the qualitie and meaſure of the offence ſhall deſerve .

Members of Court tranſgreſſing: reproof:

And if any Magiſtrate or other member of any court ſhall uſe any reproachfull, or un-beſeeming ſpeeches, or behaviour towards any Magiſtrate, Judge, or member of the Court in the face of the ſaid Court he ſhall be ſharply reproved, by the Governour, or other principal Judge of the ſame Court for the time being .

further cenſure,

And if the qualitie of the offence be ſuch as ſhall deſerve a farther cenſure, or if the perſon ſo reproved ſhall reply again without leave, the ſame Court may proceed to puniſh any ſuch offender

next ſuperior Court

by Fine, or Impriſonment , or it ſhall be preſented to, and cenſured at the next ſuperiour Court .

Offences in ye Gen: Court

2 If in a General Court any miſcarriage ſhall be amongſt the Magiſtrates when they are by themſelves, it ſhall be examined, and ſentenced amongſt themſelves. If amongſt the Deputies when they are by themſelves, it ſhall be examined, and ſentenced amongſt themſelves . If it be when the whole Court is together , it ſhall be judged by the whole Court , and not ſeverall as before. [1637 1641]

Who may call a Gen: Court

3 And it is ordered by the Authoritie of this Court that the Governour , Deputie Governour, or greater part of the Aſſiſtants may upon urgent occaſion call a General Court at any time . [1647]

4 *And wheras there may ariſe ſome difference of judgement in doubtfull caſes , it is therfore farther ordered;*

What ſhal be a valid Act

That no Law, Order, or Sentence ſhall paſſe as an Act of the Court without the conſent of the greater part of the Magiſtrates on the one partie, and the greater number of the Deputies on the other part.

5 *And for preventing all occaſions of partial and undue proceeding in Courts of juſtice, and avoyding of jealouſies which may be taken up againſt Judges in that kinde, it is farther ordered ,*

When a Magiſtrate ſhal have no vote

That in everie Caſe of civil nature between partie and partie where there ſhall fall out ſo neer relation between any Judge and any of the parties as between Father and Son , either by nature or marriage , Brother and Brother ; in like kinde Uncle and Nephew, Land-lord and Tenent in matters of conſiderable value , ſuch Judge though he may have libertie to be preſent in the Court at the time of the tryall, and give reaſonable advice in the Caſe, yet ſhall have no power to vote or give ſentence therin, neither

neither ſhall ſit as Judge , but beneath the Bench when he ſhall ſo plead or give advice in the Caſe . [1635] *See Burglary, Cauſes, Charges publ: Sect: 3, Death untimely, Drukeñes , Elections Sect: 3, Gaming , High-wayes , In-keepers , Leather , Marri-age , Maſters Servants , Oaths , Tranſportation*

Man-ſlaughter .

IT is ordered by this Court and Authoritie therof; that if any perſon in the juſt, and neceſſarie defence of his life , or the life of any other , ſhall kill any perſon attempting to rob, or murther in the field, or high-way, or to break into any dwel- | *ſe defendendo*
ling houſe if he conceive he cannot with ſafety of his own perſon otherwiſe take the Felon, or Aſſailant, or bring him to Tryall he ſhall be holden blameles . [1647]

Marriage .

FOR *preventing all unlawfull marriages , it is ordered by this Court and Authoritie therof,*

That after due publication heerof no perſons ſhall be joyned in marriage before | Three times the intention of the parties proceeding therin hath been three times publiſhed at ſome | publiſhed or time of publick Lecture or Town-meeting , in both the towns where the parties or ei- | poſted four ther of them doe ordinarily reſide ; or be ſet up in writing upon ſome poſt of their | teen dayes Meeting-houſe door in publick view , there to ſtand ſo as it may eaſily be read by the ſpace of fourteen dayes . [1639]

2 *And wheras God hath committed the care and power into the hands of Parents for the diſpoſing their Children in marriage : ſo that it is againſt Rule to ſeek to draw away the affections of young maidens under pretence of purpoſe of marriage before their Parents have given way and allowance in that reſpect . And wheras it is a common practice in divers places for young men irregularly and diſorderly to watch all advantages for their evil purpoſes to inſinuate into the affections of young maidens , by coming to them in places , and ſeaſons unknown to their Parents, for ſuch ends; wherby much evil hath grown amongſt us to the diſhonour of God and damage of parties , for prevention wherof for time to come it is farther ordered by Authoritie of this Court ,*

That whatſoever perſon from henceforth ſhall indeavour directly , or indirectly | No pretence to draw away the affections of any maid in this Juriſdiction under pretence of marriage, | of marriage before he hath obtained libertie and allowance from her Parents or Governours (or in | to any maid abſence of ſuch) of the neereſt Magiſtrate ; he ſhall forfeit for the firſt offence five | without con-pounds , for the ſecond offence toward the ſame partie ten pounds , and be bound to | ſent of Parents forbear any farther attempt and proceedings in that unlawfull deſigne without , or a- | on payn of 5 li gainſt the allowance aforeſaid . And for the third offence upon information, or com- | firſt offence, plaint by ſuch Parents or Governours to any Magiſtrate, giving *Bond* to proſecute the | Sec: offence partie, he ſhall be committed to priſon, and upon hearing and conviction by the next | 10 li. and Court ſhall be adjudged to continue in priſon untill the Court of Aſſiſtants ſhall ſee cauſe | good behavi-to releaſe him . [1647] | our, Third offen: impriſoned.

3 *Wheras divers perſons both men and woemen living within this Juriſdiction whoſe Wives, and Husbands are in England, or elſ-where, by means wherof they live under great temptations heer, and ſome of them committing lewdnes and filthines heer among us, others make love to woemen, and attempt Marriage, and ſome have attained it; and ſome of them live under ſuſpicion of uncleannes , and all to the great diſhonour of God , re-proach of Religion, Common-wealth and Churches, it is therfore ordered by this Court & Authoritie therof (for the prevention of all ſuch future evils)*

That all ſuch married perſons as aforeſaid ſhall repair to their ſaid relations by the | Mar: perſons firſt opportunitie of ſhipping upon the pain, or penaltie of twenty pounds, except they | to go to their can ſhew juſt cauſe to the contrary to the next County Court, or Court of Aſſiſtants to | Wives on pain be holden at *Boſton* after they are ſummoned by the Conſtable there to appear , who | of 20 li. are heerby required ſo to doe upon pain of twenty ſhillings for everie ſuch default wit- | except they tingly made . Provided that this Order doe not extend to ſuch as are come over to | ſhew cauſe. make way for their families, or are in a tranſient way only for traffick, or merchandize | Conſtable to for ſome ſmall time . [1647] | Summon on pain of 20 ſs | Caution.

F

4 *As the Ordinance of Marriage is honourable amongst all so should it be accordingly*
solemnized .   It is therfore ordered by this Court and Authoritie therof;

Who may
solemnize
marriage.

That no perfon whatfoever in this Jurifdiction fhall joyn any perfons together in
Marriage but the Magiftrate, or fuch other as the General Court, or Court of Affiftants
fhall authorize in fuch places where no Magiftrate is neer .   Nor fhall any joyn themfelves in Marriage but before fome Magiftrate , or perfon authorized as aforefaid.

not before due
publication.

Nor fhall any Magiftrate, or other perfon authorized as aforefaid joyn any perfons together in Marriage, or fuffer them to joyn together in Marriage in their prefence before
the parties to be married have been publifhed according to Law . [1648] *See Children*
Sect: 3. 4.

Marshal.

F ORASMUCH *as delay in executing juftice is dangerous to any State , and wher-*
as many offenders are punifhed only by Fines or pecuniarie Mulcts; if there be delay
or neglect in Officers, that fuch Fines and Penalties are not duly levied, then fin is unpu-
nifhed, the Name and Ordinance of God may thereby be reproached,   it is therfore or-
dered by this Court and Authoritie therof;

All fines payd
prefently or
fecuritie given

That everie offender that fhall at any time be fined for the breach of any pænal
Law, fuch perfon or perfons fo offending fhall forthwith pay his or their Fine or Penaltie , or put in fecuritie fpeedily to doe it , or elfe fhall be imprifoned , or kept to
work till it be payd that no loffe may come to the Common-wealth :   and what other

The Marfhal
by war: frõ ỹ
Treafurer to
levie all fines
on pain of twõ
fhil: ỹ pound
or fine.

fines or debts be already due, or fhall be due to the Countrie the Marfhal for the time
being upon *Warrant* from the Treafurer, and according to his oath fhall be faithfull
in doing the duties of his place , in levying, and returning of the fame upon pain of
forfeiting two fhillings out of his own eftate for everie pound , or elfe fuch Fine as any
Court of juftice fhall impofe on him for his neglect. [1646]   *See Actions, Caufes,*
Clerk of Writs, Oaths.

Masters, Servants, Labourers.

No fervant
fhall give or
truck with-
out his Mafters
leave
Corporal pu-
nifhment or
Fine.

I T is ordered by this Court and the Authoritie therof, that no fervant, either man
or maid fhall either give, fell or *truck* any commoditie whatfoever without licence
from their Mafters, during the time of their fervice under pain of Fine, or corporal punifhment at the difcretion of the Court as the offence fhall deferve.

How long men
fhall work.

2 And that all workmen fhall work the whole day allowing convenient time for
food and reft .

Purfuit after
fervants or
Inhabit: fled.
Impreffe

3 It is alfo ordered that when any fervants fhall run from their mafters, or any
other Inhabitants fhall privily goe away with fufpicion of ill intentions , it fhall be
lawfull for the next Magiftrate, or the Conftable and two of the chief Inhabitants
where no Magiftrate is to preffe men and boats or pinnaces at the publick charge to pur-
fue fuch perfons by Sea or Land and bring them back by force of Arms .

Wages to be
fer by towns,

4 It is alfo ordered by the Authoritie aforefaid , that the Free-men of everie town
may from time to time as occafion fhall require agree amongft themfelves about the
prizes, and rates of all workmens labours and fervants wages .   And everie perfon inhabiting in any town, whether workman, labourer or fervant fhall be bound to the
fame rates which the faid Freemen, or the greater part fhall binde themfelves unto:

Penaltie for
giving or tak:
more wages.
If towns diffr.
County court
decide it

and whofoever fhall exceed thofe rates fo agreed fhall be punifhed by the difcretion of
the Court of that Shire, according to the qualitie and meafure of the offence .   And
if any town fhall have caufe of complaint againft the Freemen of any other town for
allowing greater rates, or wages then themfelves, the Quarter Court of that Shire fhall
from time to time fet order therin .

wherin wages
may de paid
and how to
be valued.

5 And for fervants and workmens wages, it is ordered, that they may be paid in
corn, to be valued by two indifferent Freemen, chofen the one by the Mafter, the
other by the fervant or workman, who alfo are to have refpect to the value of the work
or fervice, and if they cannot agree then a third man fhall be chofen by the next Magiftrate, or if no Magiftrate be in the town then by the next Conftable, unles the par-

Provifo for
fpec· cõtracts

ties agree the price themfelves .   Provided if any fervant or workman agree for any
particular

particular payment, then to be payd *in ſpecie*, or conſideration for default therin. And for all other payments in corn, if the parties cannot agree they ſhall chooſ two indifferent men, and if they cannot agree then a third as before.

6 It is ordered, and by this Court declared, that if any ſervant ſhall flee from the tyrannie and crueltie of his, or her Maſter to the houſe of any Freeman of the ſame town, they ſhall be there protected and ſuſteined till due order be taken for their releif. Provided due notice therof be ſpeedily given to their Maſter from whom they fled, and to the next Magiſtrate or Conſtable where the partie ſo fled is harboured.

7 Alſo that no ſervant ſhall be put off for above a year to any other, neither in the life time of their Maſter, nor after their death by their Executors or Adminiſtrators, unles it be by conſent of Authorite aſſembled in ſome Court, or two Aſſiſtants: otherwiſe all, and everie ſuch Aſſignment to be void in Law.

8 And that if any man ſmite out the eye, or tooth of his man-ſervant, or maid-ſervant; or otherwiſe maim, or much disfigure them (unles it be by meer caſualtie) he ſhall let them goe free from his ſervice, and ſhall allow ſuch farther recompence as the Court ſhall adjudge him.

9 And all ſervants that have ſerved diligently and faithfully to the benefit of their Maſters ſeven years ſhall not be ſent away emptie: and if any have been unfaithfull, negligent, or unprofitable in their ſervice, notwithſtanding the good uſage of their Maſters, they ſhall not be diſmiſſed till they have made ſatisfaction according to the judgement of Authoritie. [1630 1633 1635 1636 1641] *See Oppreſſion.*

Militarie Affairs.

*F*ORASMUCH *as the wiſe, and well mannaging the Militia of this Commonwealth is a matter of great concernment, therefore that it may be carried an end with the utmoſt ſafety and certaintie for the beſt benefit of the Countrie, it is ordered by this Court and Authoritie therof;*

That henceforth there ſhall be one Sergeant Major of everie Regiment choſen by the trained ſoldiers of everie Town in each Shire, not only Freemen, but all others that have taken, and ſhall take the Oath of fidelitie (except unſetled perſons) who upon *Warrant* from the General Court, or Sergeant Major General ſhall meet together in their ſeveral Towns from time to time, and give in their Votes for ſuch a man, or men as they ſhall judge fit for the Office of Sergeant Major of that Regiment, and where no Magiſtrate is in the Town, or neer hand to give Oath to ſuch ſoldiers as deſire to take the ſame before the Election, power is heerby given to the Captain, or in defect therof to the next cheif Officer of the Company in all Towns to adminiſter the ſaid Oath of fidelitie; who ſhall certifie the next Court of that County the names of all ſoldiers ſo ſworn to be recorded there: which Votes of the whole Company ſhall be ſealed up, and delivered to one, or both the Deputies of the ſaid Town, or any other Freeman that the Town ſhall appoint to carie them to the Shire town of each County at ſuch time as the *Warrant* ſhall direct, and there before one or two of the neereſt Magiſtrates to open the *Proxies* with the ſaid Deputies or Freemen. And he that ſhall have the greater number of Votes, being a Freeman, ſhall be preſented by one of the ſaid Magiſtrates of each Shire unto the Sergeant Major General within one week after the Election, who ſhall enſtall, confirm and eſtabliſh each Sergeant Major in his place for one year, who ſhall alſo retein their place and power, till a new Election be made by the General Court, or otherwiſe according to this Order. And to avoid the vacancy of a place ſo neceſſarie for time to come, it is ordered, that if any ſuch Officer leave their places, or be removed out of them the Sergeant Major General for the time being ſhall within one month at the fartheſt after ſuch a change ſend forth his *Warrants* to each town in the ſame Shire to make choiſ of one or more for Majors according to the form afore-mentioned.

2 And it is farther ordered, that everie Sergeant Major not only hath libertie, but

F 2   alſo

Margin notes:

Corn, how to be prized in all payments.

Servants flying frō Maſters cruelty releiv:

proviſo for due notice

Servants not put off without licence Two Magiſtr:

Servants maimed &c. Diſcharged.

Faithful ſervants recompenced, unfaithful fined, deteined

Serg: Major how to be choſen.

Oath of fidelitie.

where no Magiſtrate is y̌ cheif Officer may give the Oath

Serg: Major Gen: ſhal enſtall him continue til new choſen.

Najor Gen: to provide for ſupply &c:

Everie Regiment to train once a year at com: of the Major Gener:

alſo is heerby injoyned once everie year at leaſt , and oftener upon any needfull occaſion, or command from the Major General to draw forth his Regiment into one convenient place , and there to put everie Captain and Officer of their Companyes in their places , and to inſtruct them in their duties according to the rules of militarie Diſciplin, and to exerciſe his Regiment, whether it ſhall confiſt of Horſe, Pikes or Musketiers according to his beſt skill and abilities as if he were to lead them forth againſt an enemie . *And* farther, that everie Sergeant Major not only hath power , but is injoyned by the Court twice everie year to ſend forth his *Warrants* or *Summons* to require the

The chief Officers of everie Regim: to meet twice a year by war: from ẏ Major for what ends

chief Officers of each Company in his Regiment to meet at ſuch time and place as he ſhall appoint , and there, with them to confer, and give in command ſuch Orders as ſhall by them be judged meet for the better ordering and ſetling their particular Companyes in militarie Exerciſes: and that theſe Officers of particular Companyes ſhall bring with them a note from the *Rolls* of their ſeverall Clerks of the names of ſuch in their ſeveral Companyes as remain delinquents, and have not given ſatisfaction to the Captain, or cheif Officers of their Companyes for all defects either in their arms, amunition, appearances, watches, offences, or the like . And that the Sergeant Major with the conſent of thoſe Officers, then met together, ſhall impoſe ſuch Fines or Penal-

puniſh delinquents.

ties according to Law upon delinqents as ſhall be judged equal , and ſhall give order to the Clerks of the ſeverall Bands to take *diſtreſſe* for the ſame, within one month after ſuch order, if before, they give not ſatisfaction.

3 *And becauſe ẇe obſerve and underſtand many defects to be in making appearances , in Arms unfit for ſervice and otherẇiſe , ẇe order that it ſhall be inſerted into the Oath of everie Clerk of the Band as folloẇeth,*

Clerk of Band, his duty.

Firſt, that upon everie training day twice, once in the forenoon, as alſo in the after-noon at ſuch time as the Captain, or cheif Officer that is then in the field ſhall appoint to call, or cauſe to be called over the Liſt of the names of all the ſoldiers ; and that he ſhall give his attendance in the field all the day (except he have ſpecial leave from his Captain, or chief Officer) for the taking notice of any defect by the abſence of ſoldiers, and other offences that doe often fall out in the time of Exerciſe , as well as in the calling over of the *Rolls* .

Secondly, that twice everie year, at leaſt, he ſhall view all the Arms and Amunition of the Band to ſee if they be all according to Law : to which end, by direction of the Captain, or chief Officer of the Band he ſhall give notice to the ſoldiers that upon ſuch a training day appointed, they be required to bring (in the fore-noon) all their Arms and Amunition into the field that is required by Law; where they ſhall be approved or diſ-allowed by the judgements of the ſaid chief Officers then in the field. Alſo, the Clerk ſhall ſee that everie *Musketier* have one pound of powder , twenty *bullets* and two fathom of *match*, with *Musket, Sword, Bandeliers* and *Reſt,* upon the penalty of ten ſhillings for everie defect . And to levie five ſhillings forfeit upon all ſoldiers that ſhall be abſent from training, or defective in watching and warding, except they be diſcharged, or their Fine mittigated in any the particulars afore-mentioned, by the chief Officers of the Company . And that the Clerk as often as he ſhall ſee occaſion is injoyned to uſe all diligence to view everie ones Arms, whether they be compleatly furniſhed with all Arms and Amunition that the Law requireth .

Thirdly, he ſhall ſee that all Inhabitants, as well Sea-men as others have *A*rms in their houſes fit for ſervice , with *Poẇder, Bullets, Match* and other amunition as other ſoldiers : and that Fiſhermen, Ship-carpenters and all others, not exempted by Law (except *Deacons,* who heerby are freed from watching and warding) ſhall watch or provide a ſufficient Watch-man in their room, and to train twice a year according to the Order .

milit: Officers appoint what Arms.

Fourthly, that the militarie Officers of each Company ſhall appoint what arms everie ſoldier ſhall ſerve with, ſo that there be two thirds *Muskets,* and thoſe which ſerve with *Pikes* to have their *Corſlets* and *Head-pieces* .

Fiftly, that the Clerk ſhall within one week after everie training day truly
preſent

prefent a Lift of the names of all that are delinquents, and of the defects of the Band to the Captain, or chief Officer of the Company, that he may have them all in a readines to carrie with him when the Major of the Regiment fhall appoint his meeting, which have not before given fatisfaction at home, according to Law. And the Order that gives power to Magiftrates to releaf upon non-appearance is heerby repealed.

      Sixtly, that the Clerk (without all partialitie) fhall demand, and receive all Fines, which if any fhall refufe to pay, then he fhall make *diftreffe* upon the goods of all fuch perfons as firft by the chief Officer of their own Company at home, or by the Major and chief Officers met together *(as before mentioned)* fhall be judged delinquents. And that the Clerk with the advife of the chief Officers of their own company fhall fpeedily lay out all Fines received either in *Enfigne*, *Drum*, *Halberds*, candle, or wood for their Court of Guard, or to provide *Powder* or *Arms* for the poorer fort, or otherwife for the ufe of the Company. Provided, that no Clerk of the Band fhall ftand charged with the execution of any former Order by vertue of his faid Office, other then fuch as are committed to his care and charge by this prefent Order.

      Laftly, if any Clerk of a Band, chofen, fhall refufe either to accept the place, or to take his Oath, he fhall pay to the ufe of the Company fourty fhillings, and the Company fhall choof another, and all that refufe the faid Place, or Oath as before fhall pay fourty fhillings a peece till one doth accept the Place. And he that doth hold the Place fhall have a fourth part of the Fines for his labour.

     4 *For the militarie Watch in all Towns it is ordered*;

      Firft, that the Watch fhall be fet and have their charge by the direction of the chief militarie Officers of that place, half an hour after fun-fetting.

      Secondly, that the Watch being fet [which fhall ftand double, a *Pike* and a *Musket* together] fhall examin all perfons that they fhall meet withall within the compaffe of their Watch or Round: and all fuch as they fufpect they fhall carry to the Court of Guard there to be kept untill the morning, and before they be difmiffed they fhall carrie them to their chief Officers to be examined and proceeded with according to Law.

      Thirdly, if the Centinel, or Watch fhall meet with fuch perfons as fhall prove too ftrong for them, or by their carriage fhall give juft caufe of fufpicion, or will not fubmit to their command, or if they fhall either draw upon them, or offer any fuch affronts, in words or actions as fhall put them in fear or hazzard of their lives, they fhall charge their *Pike* and difcharge their *Musket* upon them, and return with fpeed to their Court of Guard and raife an Alarm. Provided alwayes that in times of peace when the Council of war, or the chief Officers of any Company fhall not apprehend danger by the neernes of an enemie, it fhall not be in the libertie of any Centinel to hazzard the killing of any perfon, or perfons, except in his own neceffarie defence, but if the caufe require it he fhall raife an Alarm, or retire to the Court of Guard.

     5 *For the well ordering of the militarie Companies and affairs throughout this Jurifdiction it is ordered by this Court and Authoritie therof*;

      That the militarie Officers of each Company upon three or four dayes warning or more, in any publick Meeting, or otherwife in their own Town fhall from time to time appoint the dayes for training their Companies; fo as there be eight dayes appointed for the fame everie year, and none of them to be in the fift or fixth months.

     Alfo, it is ordered, for eafe of all foldiers when, and where the Regiments are exercifed,

      That fo many dayes as they fhall neceffarily expend by the injunction of the Sergeant Major, both in marching to and from exercife at General trainings, fhall be deducted out of their eight dayes annual trainings.

      And that all Magiftrats, Deputies, and Officers of court, Elders and Deacons, the Prefident, Fellows, Students and Officers of *Harvard-Colledge*, and all profeffed School-mafters, allowed by any two Magiftrates, the Treafurer, Auditor general and Surveyor General of the Arms, Publick Notaries, Phyfitians and Chirurgions,

F 3   allowed

Marginal notes:

Clerk to prefent defects within one week.

Clerks duty about fines

How fines fhall be imployed.

The Clerk not charged wt any former Orders

refufing to be Clerk &c

fourty fhillings fine fourth part of ỹ fines to the Clerk milit: watch how to be ordered.

Caution for prevᵗ. Manflaughter

Who fhall appoint training dayes

Dayes of gen: training deducted frõ the 8 dayes of tee Company

perfons exempt from trainings.

Any Court may difcharge upon caufe

whofe fons & fervants fhal be exempted.

Major Gĕ.

perfons exempt fhal have Arms except.

who have vote in election of mil: Officers to be allowed by the next Coŭ: court

where Arms cañot be had

want of ability to bring Arms

affize of muskets & their furniture

Snap-fack.

Smiths &c: attĕd repair for country pay &c: Penalty five pounds. Pen: ten fhil:

Suveyor Gĕ: may fell country Arms Town Arms fafely kept pen: 10 fs. the week.

Bring arms to Meet: houfes

Secur: Arms at Farms Exercifing youth &c:

mili: watches in time of danger. Shooting in night Penalty 40 fs.

allowed by two Magiftrates, Mafters of fhipps and other veffels above twenty tunnes, Millers and conftant Heards-men, and fuch other as by any Court fhall be difcharged, either for bodily infirmity, or other reafonable caufe fhall be exempt from ordinary trainings, and from watchings and wardings but not their fons or fervants, fave one fervant of everie Magiftrate and Teaching Elder allowed exemption : and all fuch as keep families at remote Farms fhall not be compellable to fend their fervants to watch and ward in Towns . And the fons, and houfhold fervants of the Major General for the time being fhall be exercifed by his own order , and not otherwife compellable to attend the ordinary trainings . But all perfons whatfoever exempted as aforefaid, except Magiftrates and Teaching Elders fhall be provided of Arms and Amunition, as other men are .

6 Alfo that everie foldier Lifted in any trayned Band, having taken the Oath of fidelitie , and everie Freeman (though not fo lifted) fhall have his Vote in nomination of militarie Officers of that Company, or Town whereof he is , provided they be Freemen . And everie Captain, Lievtenant and Enfigne fo nominated fhall be prefented to the next County Court to be allowed .

7 And if any perfon who is by Law to provide Arms or Amunition cannot purchafe them by fuch means as he hath , he fhall bring to the Clerk fo much corn, or other merchantable goods as by apprizement of the faid Clerk and two others of the Company (wherof one to be chofen by the partie) fhall be adjudged of greater value, by a fift part then fuch Arms or Amunition is of, he fhall be excufed of the penaltie for want of Arms (but not for want of appearance) untill he be provided . And the Clerk fhall indeavour to furnifh him fo foon as may be by fale of fuch goods fo depofited, rendring the partie the overplus . But if any perfon fhall not be able to provide himfelfe Arms or Amunition through meer povertie , if he be fingle, he fhall be put to fervice by fome Magiftrate , & the Conftable fhall provide him Arms and Amunition , and fhall appoint him when, and with whom to earn it out .

8 Alfo, that no *Musket* fhall be allowed for fervice under baftard musket bore, and not under three foot nine inches in length , nor any piece above four foot three inches long . And everie fuch foldier fhall be furnifhed with a priming wyer, Worm, Scourer and Mould, fitted to the bore of his *Musket* : and everie foldier with a Snap-fack .

9 It is alfo ordered by the Authoritie aforefaid ; that upon any militarie expedition upon occafion of an enemie all Smiths and other needfull Workmen fhall attend the repairing of Arms , and other neceffaries : for which they fhall not refufe fuch pay as the Countrie affords upon pain of five pounds for everie fuch neglect . And for fuch neglect at any other time more then ten dayes , to forfeit for everie fuch offence ten fhillings .

10 Alfo, power is given to the Surveyor general to fell any of the common Arms, when he feeth occafion .

11 And everie Town which fhall have any arms or amunition belonging to the common Store of the Town fhall provide a meet place to keep the fame in ; and fhall fafely preferve the fame upon pain of ten fhillings for everie weeks default therin .

12 Alfo, the militarie Officers of everie Company in fuch places and at fuch times as they fhall apprehend danger from an enemie, fhall have power to order the foldiers of their Companies what arms to bring to the Meeting-houfes , at the times of the publick Affemblies : and to take order for the fecuring the arms and amunition at remote Farms . Alfo, in everie Company fome under Officer fhall be appointed by the cheif Commander to exercife fuch children as by their Parents and Mafters allowance fhall refort to the Traynings .

13 It is alfo ordered, that in the times of danger the watches & wards fhal be fet by the militarie Officers in fuch places as they fhall judge moft convenient, and if any man fhall fhoot off a gun after fuch watch is fet (except in cafe of Alarm) he fhall forfeit to the Treafurie fourty fhillings. *See Watches.*

14 And

14 And for an Alarm, either the diſtinct diſcharge of three *Muskets* or the continued beat of the *Drum* or the fyring of a *Beacon*, or diſcharge of a Piece of *Ordnance* and two *Muskets* after it , or any of theſe in the night ; or the ſending of a meſſenger on purpoſe to give notice of an enemie at hand ſhall be accounted a general Alarm, which everie trayned Soldier is to take immediately, on pain of five pounds. And beſides the ſaid general Alarm there ſhall be a ſpecial Alarm for the Town *viz:* one *Musket* diſcharged, which the Centinell ſhall anſwer by going to all the houſes in his quarters and crying arm, arm . And if the danger appear the chief Officers may either ſtrengthen their quarters, or give a general Alarm ; and they ſhal ſet their Centinels or Courts of guard where they ſhall judge moſt convenient : and upon certain intelligence of an enemie at one Town, the Commanders of the three next Towns ſhall repair thither with a ſufficient company according to the intelligence given them of the enemies ſtrength .

15 Alſo any three chief Officers of each company ſhall heerby have power to puniſh ſuch Soldiers as ſhall commit any diſorder, or contempt upon any day, or time of militarie exerciſe , or upon any Watch or Ward by *Stocks* , *Bilboes* or any other uſuall military puniſhment, or by Fine, not exceeding twenty ſhillings, or may commit ſuch offender to the Conſtable to be carried before ſome Magiſtrate, who may binde him over to the next Court of that Shire if the cauſe ſo require, or cõmit him to priſon.

16 It is heerby declared, that it belongeth to the place of the Governour for the time being to be General of all the militarie Forces . But when occaſion of ſervice ſhal be againſt an enemie , the General Court or ſtanding Council may appoint ſome other to that Office untill the Forces rayſed ſhall be disbanded .

17 Laſtly , every Town ſhall provide a ſufficient Watch-houſe before the laſt of the fifth month next upon pain of five pounds . [1645 1647] *See Council* .

Mills, Millers.

IT is ordered by this Court and Authoritie therof, that no Miller ſhall take above the ſixteenth part of the corn he grindes . And that everie Miller ſhall have allwayes ready in his mill, weights and skoals provided at his own charges, to weigh corn to and from mill, if men deſire it . [1635 1638]

Monopolies .

IT is ordered, decreed and by this Court declared ; that there ſhall be no *Monopolies* graunted or allowed amongſt us, but of ſuch new inventions that are profitable for the Countrie , and that for a ſhort time . [1641]

Oaths , Subſcription

IT is ordered and decreed, and by this Court declared ; that no man ſhall be urged to take any oath, or ſubſcribe any Articles, Covenants, or remonſtrance of publick and civil nature but ſuch as the General Court hath conſidered, allowed and required. And that no oath of Magiſtrate, Counceller or any other Officer ſhall binde him any farther, or longer then he is reſident, or reputed an Inhabitant of this Juriſdictiõ [1641]

Oppreſſion

FOR avoyding ſuch miſcheifs as may follow by ſuch ill diſpoſed perſons as may take libertie to oppreſſe and wrong their neighbours, by taking exceſſive wages for work , or unreaſonable prizes for ſuch neceſſarie merchandizes or other commodities as ſhall paſſe from man to man, it is ordered , That if any man ſhall offend in any of the ſaid caſes he ſhall be puniſhed by Fine, or Impriſonment according to the qualitie of the offence, as the Court to which he is preſented upon lawfull tryall & conviction ſhall adjudge . [1635]

Payments .

IT is ordered by the Authoritie of this Court, that all payments of Debt, Legacyes and Fines ſhall be ſatisfied in kinde according to covenant or ingagement , or in default therof in corn, cattle, fiſh or other cõmodities at ſuch rates as this Court ſhall appoint from time to time , or by apprizement of indifferent men to be appointed by the Officer one , and either partie one . Provided that in all and everie the caſes aforeſaid

---

Margin notes:

What ſhall be a gen: Alarm Every trained Soldier muſt take it Penaltie, five poud What, a ſpecial Alarm what, to be done upon it.

Three chief Officers may puniſh contempts &c: upon trayning days, or watches and wards or ſend the offender to a Magiſtr: The Gover: General.

watch-houſ in everie town.

Toll. weights & skoals.

How far publ: oaths binde.

Satisfaction according to covenant.

aforeſaid all juſt damages ſhall be ſatisfied together with the debt , or other payment to the partie for not paying in kinde according to the bargain . [1640]

Pipe-ſtaves .

WHERAS *information hath come to this Court from divers forrein parts of the inſufficiencie of our Pipe-ſtaves in regard eſpecially of worm holes, wherby the commoditie is like to be prohibited in thoſe parts, to the great damage of the Countrie ; it is therfore ordered and enacted by the Authoritie of this Court ,*

Searchers of Pipe-ſtaves

That the Select-men of *Boſton* and *Charlſtown* and of all other towns in this Juriſdiction where Pipe-ſtaves uſe to be ſhipped ; ſhall forthwith, and ſo from time to time as need ſhall require nominate two men of each town, skilfull in that commoditie, and ſuch as can attend that ſervice to be Viewers of Pipe-ſtaves ; who ſo choſen, ſhall

ſworn.

by the Conſtable be convented before ſome Magiſtrate, to be ſworn diligently and faithfully to view and ſearch all ſuch Pipe-ſtaves as are to be tranſported to any parts of *Spain* , *Portugal,* or within either of their Dominions , or elſewhere to be uſed for making of tight cask, who ſhall caſt bye all ſuch as they ſhall judge not merchantable

Aſſize of Pipe-ſtaves

both in reſpect of worm-holes and due aſſize *viz* that are not in length four foot & half, in breadth three inches and half without ſap , in thicknes three quarters of an inch, & not more or leſſe then an eight part of an inch then three quarters thick : well, and

attend, Regiſter.

even hewed and ſufficient for that uſe . And they or ſome one of them ſhall at all times upon requeſt give attendance ; & they ſhall enter in a book the number of all ſuch merchantable Pipe-ſtaves as they ſhall approve , and for whom .

Owners ſhipping ũlawfull Pipeſtaves. Drie cask Forfeit. Searchers allowance.

And if any man ſhall put aboard any Ship, or other veſſel any Pipe-ſtaves other then ſhall be ſo ſearched and approved , to the end to be tranſported to any part of *Spain* or *Portugal,* except they ſhould be ſhipped for dry cask, he ſhall forfeit the ſame whole parcell or the value therof ; and the ſaid Viewers ſhall be allowed two ſhillings for everie thouſand of Pipe-ſtaves which they ſhall ſo ſearch , as well the refuſe as the merchantable , to be paid by him that ſets them a work .

Maſter, ſhipping ũlawfull Pipe-ſtaves

And if any Maſter or other Officer of any Ship , or other veſſel ſhall receive into ſuch Ship or veſſel any parcel of Pipe-ſtaves to be tranſported into any of the ſaid Dominions which ſhall not be ſearched , and allowed as merchantable , and ſo certified by a note under the hand of one of the ſaid Viewers ſuch Maſter ſhall forfeit for everie

Forfeit.

thouſand of Pipe-ſtaves ſo unduly received five pounds ; except he can procure one of the ſaid Viewers to come aboard and ſearch ſuch ſtaves as they ſhall be delivered into the Ship .

Dry cask.

Provided, cask ſtaves or other red oak ſtaves may be tranſported into thoſe parts, which may be of good uſe for drye cask . And that there be the like Officers choſen for *Salem* and *Peſcataway*, where ſtaves may be ſhipped away as well as from *Boſton* [1646]

Poor .

To be ſetled where, & by whom.

IT is ordered by this Court and Authoritie therof ; that any Shire Court, or any two Magiſtrates out of Court ſhall have power to determin all differences about lawfull ſetling , and providing for poor perſons : and ſhall have power to diſpoſe of all unſetled perſons into ſuch towns as they ſhall judge to be moſt fit for the maintainance, and imployment of ſuch perſons and families , for the eaſe of the Countrie. [1639]

Pound, Pound breach .

FOR *prevention, and due recompence of damages in corn fields , and other incloſures, done by ſwine and cattle, it is ordered by this Court and Authoritie therof*;

That there ſhall be one ſufficient Pound, or more made and maintained in everie Town and Village within this Juriſdiction , for the impounding of all ſuch ſwine and cattle as ſhall be found in any corn field or other incloſure . And who ſo impounds any ſwine or cattle ſhall give preſent notice to the Owner, if he be known , otherwiſe they ſhal be cryed at the two next Lectures or Markets, and if ſwine or cattle eſcape out of pound the owners, if known, ſhal pay all damages according to law. [1645 1647]

2   *Wheras impounding of cattle in cafe of trespaſſe hath been alwayes found both needfull and profitable, and all breaches about the fame very offenfive and injurious, it is therfore ordered by this Court and Authoritie therof;*

That if any perſon ſhall reſiſt, or reſcue any cattle going to the *Pound*, or ſhall by any way or means convey them out of *pound* or other cuſtodie of the Law, whereby the partie wronged may loſe his damages, and the Law be deluded, that in cafe of meer *refcues* the partie ſo offending ſhall forfeit to the Treaſurie fourty ſhillings. And in cafe of pound breach five pounds, and ſhall alſo pay all damages to the partie wronged, and if in the *refcues* any bodily harm be done to the perſon of any man or other, they may have remedie againſt the *Refcuers*; and if either be done by any not of abilitie to anſwer the Forfeiture and damages aforeſaid, they ſhall be openly whipped, by *War-rant* from any Magiſtrate before whom the offender is convicted, in the Town or Plantation where the offence was committed, not exceeding twenty ſtripes for the meer *refcues* or pound breach. And for all damages to the partie they ſhall ſatisfie by ſervice as in cafe of theft. And if it appear there were any procurement of the Owner of the cattle therunto, and that they were *Abbettors* therin, they ſhall alſo pay Forfeiture and damages as if themſelves had done it. [1647]

Refcues fimpl
Fine.
Pound breach. Fine. Refcues with Battery.
Whipped. one Magiftr:
damage fatis-fied by ferv:

Powder.

IT is ordered by this Court and the Authoritie therof, that whoſoever ſhall tranſport any *Gun-powder* out of this Juriſdiction without licence firſt obtained from ſome two of the Magiſtrates, ſhall forfeit for everie ſuch offence all ſuch *powder* as ſhall be tranſporting or tranſported, or the value therof. And that there may be noe defect for want of an Officer to take care therabouts, this Court, the Court of Aſſiſtants, or any Shire Court ſhall appoynt meet perſons from time to time in all needfull places, who have heerby power graunted them, to ſearch all perſons and veſſels that are, or any way ſhall be ſuſpicious to them to be breakers of the Court Order in this reſpect, and what they finde in any veſſel, or hands without order, as aforeſaid, to keep the one half to their own uſe, in recompence of their pains and vigilancy, the other half forthwith to deliver to the Treaſurer. [1645] *See Indians*.

Searchers for powder.
Forfeit di-vided,

Prefcriptions.

IT is ordered, decreed, and by this Court declared; that no *Cuſtom* or *Prefcription* ſhall ever prevail amongſt us in any moral cafe [our meaning is] to maintein any thing that can be proved to be morally ſinfull by the Word of God. [1641]

Not for evil.

Prifoners, Prifons.

IT is ordered by Authoritie of this Court; that ſuch malefactors as are committed to any common *Prifon* ſhall be conveyed thither at their own charge, if they be able, otherwiſe at the charge of the Country. [1646] *See Marfhal*.

Their charges.

Profane fwearing.

IT is ordered, and by this Court decreed, that if any perſon within this Juriſdiction ſhall *fwear* raſhly and vainly either by the holy Name of God, or any other oath, he ſhall forfeit to the common Treaſurie for everie ſuch ſeverall offence ten ſhillings. And it ſhall be in the power of any Magiſtrate by *Warrant* to the Conſtable to call ſuch perſon before him, and upon ſufficient proof to paſſe ſentence, and levie the ſaid penaltie according to the uſuall order of Juſtice. And if ſuch perſon be not able, or ſhall utterly refuſe to pay the aforeſaid Fine, he ſhal be committed to the *Stocks* there to continue, not exceeding three hours, and not leſſe then one hour. [1646]

Fine, 10 fs.
Stocks.

Proteſtation contra Remonſtrance.

IT is ordered, decreed, and by this Court declared; that it is, and ſhall be the libertie of any member, or members of any Court, Council or civil Aſſemblie in cafes of making or executing any Order or Law that properly concerneth Religion, or any cauſe Capital, or Wars, or ſubſcription to any publick Articles, or Remonſtrance in cafe they cannot in judgement and conſcience conſent to that way the major Vote or Suffrage goes, to make their *contra-Remonſtrance* or *Proteſtation* in ſpeech or writing, and upon their requeſt, to have their diſſent recorded in the *Rolls* of that Court, ſo it be

Freedom of diffent.

done chriftianly and refpectively, for the manner, and the diffent only be entred without the reafons therof for avoyding tedioufnes . [1641]

Punishment.

Once for one offence. None inhumane.

I T is ordered, decreed, and by this Court declared; that no man fhall be twice fentenced by civil Juftice for one and the fame Crime, Offence or Trefpaffe . And for bodily punifhments, wee allow amongft us none that are in-humane, barbarous or cruel . [1641] *See Appearance , Torture .*

Rates, Fines .

W HERAS much wrong hath been done to the Countrie by the negligence of Conftables *in not gathering fuch Levies as they have received Warrants from the Treafurer, during their Office, it is therefore ordered*;

The Conft: levie Rates after his Offi: is expired. If defective ẙ Treafurer diftr: Conft: goods elfe himfelf payeth Town pays for Conft: remedy where one fuffers for ẙ town

That if any Conftable fhall not have gathered the Levies committed to his charge by the Treafurer then being, during the time of his Office ,   that he fhall notwithftanding the expiration of his Office have power to levie by *diftreffe* all fuch *Rates* and *Levies* .   And if he bring them not in to the old Treafurer according to his *Warrants*, the Treafurer fhall diftrein fuch Conftables goods for the fame .   And if the Treafurer fhall not fo diftrein the Conftable, he fhall be anfwerable to the Countrie for the fame. And if the Conftable be not able to make payment, it fhall be lawfull for the Treafurer, old or new, refpectively to diftrein any man, or men of that Town where the Conftables are unable for all arrerages of *Levies* .   And that man, or men upon petition to the General Court fhall have order to collect the fame again equally of the Town , with his juft damages for the fame . [1640] *See Charges publ: Conftable,   Ecclefiasticall: Fines .*

Records .

W HERAS Records of the evidence and reafons wherupon the Verdict and Judgement *in cafes doth paffe, being duly entred, and kept would be of good ufe (for prefident to pofteritie, and to fuch as fhall have juft caufe to have their caufes reviewed) , it is therfore ordered by this Court and the Authoritie therof,*

prefidents for pofteritie

Tryalls by three men their records

& Fees.

That henceforth everie Judgement given in any Court , with all the fubftantial reafons fhall be recorded in a book, to be kept to pofteritie .   And that in all Towns within this Jurisdiction where there is no Magiftrate, the three men appointed, and fworn to end fmall caufes not exceeding fourty fhillings value fhall from time to time keep a true *Record* of all fuch Caufes as fhall come before them to be determined .   And that everie Plaintiffe fhall pay one fhilling fix pence for everie Caufe fo tryed, toward the charge therof .   And that the times of their meetings be publifhed, that all may take notice therof that are concerned therin .   And alfo that in all Towns where a Magiftrate fhall end fuch fmall Caufes, he fhall keep the like *Record*, and take the like Fee of one fhilling fixpence .

One Magiftr: to record

fmall caufes tryable where

2 Alfo, it is ordered by the Authoritie aforefaid that where parties dwell in feverall Towns it fhall be in the libertie of the Plaintiffe in which Town to trie his Action .

Town records, kept by Clerk of writs his Fee. Tranfcript recorded in Coũ: Courts

3 Alfo, that heerafter the *Clerk* of the *Writs* in feverall Towns fhall record all Births and Deaths of perfons in their Towns ;   and that for everie Birth and Death they fo record they are allowed the fum of three pence: who fhall yearly deliver in to the *Recorder* of the Court belonging to the Jurisdiction where they live a true *Tranfcript* therof , together with fo many pence as there are Births and Deaths to be recorded, under the penaltie of fourty fhillings for everie fuch neglect .

4 And it is ordered by the Authoritie aforefaid that all Parents, Mafters of fervants, Executors and Adminiftrators refpectively fhall bring in, to the *Clerks* of the *Writs* in their feverall Towns the names of fuch perfons belonging to them, or any of them, as fhall either be born, or dye .   And alfo, that everie new married man fhall likewife bring in a *Certificat* of his marriage under the hand of the Magiftrate which married him to the faid *Clerk* of the *Writs*, who fhall under the penaltie of twenty fhillings deliver as aforefaid unto the *Recorder* a *Certificat* under his hand, with a penie a name, as well for the recording of marriages as the reft .   And for each neglect the perfon to whom

Births, deaths marriages certified.

done christianly and respectively, for the manner, and the diffent only be entred without the reasons therof for avoyding tediousnes. [1641]

Punishment

Once for one offence. None inhumane.

IT is ordered, decreed, and by this Court declared; that at no man shall be twice sentenced by civil Justice for one and the same Crime, Offence or Trespasse. And for bodily punishments, wee allow amongst us none that are in-humane, barbarous or cruel. [1641] See *Appearance, Torture.*

Rates, Fines.

The Const: levie Rates after his Offi: is expired. If defective ỹ Treasurer distr: Const: goods elfe himself payeth Town pays for Const: remedy where one suffers for ỹ town

WHERAS much wrong hath been done to the Countrie by the negligence of Constables in not gathering such Levies as they have received Warrants from the Treasurer, during their Office, it is therefore ordered;

That if any Constable shall not have gathered the Levies committed to his charge by the Treasurer then being, during the time of his Office, that he shall notwithstanding the expiration of his Office have power to levie by *distresse* all such *Rates* and *Levies.* And if he bring them not in to the old Treasurer according to his *Warrants,* the Treasurer shall distrein such Constables goods for the same. And if the Treasurer shall not so distrein the Constable, he shall be answerable to the Countrie for the same. And if the Constable be not able to make payment, it shall be lawfull for the Treasurer, old or new, respectively to distrein any man, or men of that Town where the Constables are unable for all arrerages of *Levies.* And that man, or men upon petition to the General Court shall, have order to collect the same again equally of the Town, with his just damages for the same. [1640] See *Charges publ: Constable, Ecclesiasticall: Fines.*

Records.

presidents for posteritie

WHERAS Records of the evidence and reasons wherupon the *Verdict* and *Judgement* in cases doth passe, being duly entred, and kept would be of good use (for president to posteritie, and to such as shall have just cause to have their causes reviewed), it is therfore ordered by this Court and the Authoritie therof,

Tryalls by ỹ three men their records

& Fees.

Ore Magistr: to record

That henceforth everie Judgement given in any Court, with all the substantial reasons shall be recorded in a book, to be kept to posteritie. And that in all Towns within this Jurisdiction where there is no Magistrate, the three men appointed, and sworn to end small causes not exceeding fourty shillings value shall from time to time keep a true *Record* of all such Causes as shall come before them to be determined. And that everie Plaintiffe shall pay one shilling six pence for everie Cause so tryed, toward the charge therof. And that the times of their meetings be published, that all may take notice therof that are concerned therin. And also that in all Towns where a Magistrate shall end such small Causes, he shall keep the like *Record,* and take the like Fee of one shilling sixpence.

small causes tryable where

2 Also, it is ordered by the Authoritie aforesaid that where parties dwell in severall Towns it shall be in the libertie of the Plaintiffe in which Town to trie his Action.

Town records, kept by Clerk of writs his Fee. Transcript recorded in Cou: Courts

3 Also, that heerafter the *Clerk* of the *Writs* in severall Towns shall record all Births and Deaths of persons in their Towns; and that for everie Birth and Death they so record they are allowed the sum of three pence: who shall yearly deliver in to the *Recorder* of the Court belonging to the Jurisdiction where they live a true *Transcript* therof, together with so many pence as there are Births and Deaths to be recorded, under the penaltie of fourty shillings for everie such neglect.

Births, deaths marriages certified.

4 And it is ordered by the Authoritie aforesaid that all Parents, Masters of servants, Executors and Administrators respectively shall bring in, to the *Clerks* of the *Writs* in their severall Towns the names of such persons belonging to them, or any of them, as shall either be born, or dye. And also, that everie new married man shall likewise bring in a *Certificat* of his marriage under the hand of the Magistrate which married him to the said *Clerk* of the *Writs,* who shall under the penaltie of twenty shillings deliver as aforesaid unto the *Recorder* a *Certificat* under his hand, with a penie a name, as well for the recording of marriages as the rest. And for each neglect the person to whom

whom it doth belong fhall forfeit as followeth *viz:* if any perfon fhall neglect to bring in a *note* or *Certificat* as aforefaid, together with three pence a name to the faid *Clerk* of the *Writs* to be recorded more then one month after fuch Birth, Death, or Marriage he fhall then pay fix pence to the faid *Clerk* : if he neglect two months twelve pence, if three months five fhillings . All which forfeits fhall be returned into the Treafury. Alfo, the Grand-Jurors may prefent all neglects of this Order .

5 It is ordered, decreed, and by this Court declared ; that everie man fhall have libertie to record in the publick *Rolls* of any Court, any teftimonie given upon oath in the fame Court, or before two Affiftants ; or any *Deed* or *Evidence* legally confirmed, there to remain *in perpetuam rei memoriam* And that everie Inhabitant of the Countrie fhal have free libertie to fearch and view any *Rolls*, *Records* or *regifters* of any Court or Office except of the Council. And to have a *Tranfcript* or *exemplification* therof written, examined and figned by the hand of the Officer of the Office, paying the appointed Fees therefore . Alfo, everie Action between partie and partie and proceedings againft delinquents in *criminal* Caufes fhall be briefly and diftinctly entred in the *rolls* of everie Court by the *Recorder* therof, that fuch Actions be not afterwards brought again to the vexation of any man . [1639 1642 1643 1644 1647] *See Conveyances fraudulent*

Replevin

IT is ordered, decreed and by this Court declared ; that everie man fhall have libertie to *replevie* his cattle or goods impounded, diftreined, feized or extended, unles it be upon Execution after judgement, and in payment of Fines . Provided he puts in good fecuritie to profecute the *Replevin*, and to fatisfie fuch demand as his Adverfarie fhall recover againft him in Law . [1641] *See Clerk of Writs* , *Prefidents*.

Schools .

IT being one chief project of that old deluder, *Satan, to keep men from the knowledge of the Scriptures , as in former times keeping them in an unknown tongue, fo in thefe later times by perfwading from the ufe of Tongues, that fo at leaft the true fenfe and meaning of the Originall might be clowded with falfe gloffes of Saint-feeming-deceivers ; and that Learning may not be buried in the graves of our fore-fathers in Church and Commonwealth, the Lord affifting our indeavours : it is therfore ordered by this Court and Authoritie therof*;

That everie Townfhip in this Jurisdiction, after the Lord hath increafed them to the number of fifty Houfholders fhall then forthwith appoint one within their Town to teach all fuch children as fhall refort to him to write and read, whofe wages fhall be paid either by the Parents or Mafters of fuch children, or by the Inhabitants in general by way of fupply, as the major part of thofe that order the *prudentials* of the Town fhall appoint . Provided that thofe which fend their children be not oppreffed by paying much more then they can have them taught for in other Towns .

2 And it is farther ordered, that where any Town fhall increafe to the number of one hundred Families or Houfholders they fhal fet upon a Grammar-School, the Mafters therof being able to inftruct youth fo far as they may be fitted for the Univerfitie . And if any Town neglect the performance heerof above one year then everie fuch town fhall pay five pounds *per annum* to the next fuch School, till they fhall perform this Order . [1647]

Secrefie .

IT is ordered, decreed, and by this Court declared ; that no Magiftrate, Juror, Officer or other man fhall be bound to inform, prefent or reveal any private crime or offence wherin there is no perill or danger to this Colonie, or any member therof, when any neceffarie tye of confcience, grounded on the word of God bindes him to fecrefie ; unles it be in cafe of teftimonie lawfully required. [1641] *See Oath Grand-Jurie.*

Secretarie .

TO the end that all *Acts of the General Court may be amply, diftinctly and more exactly drawn up, ingroffed and recorded , and the bufines of all perticular Courts may also be more duly entred, and severally recorded for publick good , it is ordered by this Court and the Authoritie therof;*

That henceforth there shall be one able, judicious man chosen at the Court of E-lection *annually* (as other general Officers are chosen) for *Secretarie* of the General Court. And that all other Courts shal choof their own Officers frō time to time. [1647]

Ships , Ship-masters .

WHERAS *now the Countrie is in hand with the building of Ships , which is a busines of great importance for the Common good, and therfore suitable care is to be taken that it be well performed according to the commendable course of England and other places, it is therefore ordered by this Court and the Authoritie therof;*

Surveyor appointed for veſſels above 30 tuns,

That when any Ship is to be built within this Jurisdiction, or any veſſell above thirty tuns, the Owner, or builder in his abſence ſhall before they begin to plank, repair to the Governour or Deputie-Governour, or any two Magiſtrates upon the penaltie of ten pounds , who ſhall appoint ſome able man to ſurvey the work and workmen from

his power.

time to time as is uſual in England . And the ſame ſo appointed ſhall have ſuch liber-tie and power as belongs to his office . And if any Ship-carpenter ſhall not upon his advice reform and amend any thing which he ſhall finde to be amiſſe, then upon com-plaint to the Governour or Deputie Governour or any other two Magiſtrates, they ſhall

Two Ship-carpenters choſen and ſworn, their office,

appoint two of the moſt ſufficient Ship-carpenters of this Juriſdiction, and ſhall autho-rize them from time to time as need ſhall require to take view of everie ſuch ſhip, and all works thereto belonging , and to ſee that it be performed and caried on according to the rules of their Art . And for this end an oath ſhall be adminiſtred to them to be faithfull and indifferent between the Owner and the Workmen ; and their charges

their charges.

ſhall be born by ſuch as ſhall be found in default . And thoſe Viewers ſhall have power to cauſe any bad timbers, or other inſufficient work or materials to be taken out, and amended at the charge of them through whoſe default it grows . [1641 1647]

Freedom for forrein ſhips

2 It is ordered by the Authoritie of this Court, that all ſhips which come for trading only, from other parts, ſhall have free acceſſe into our Harbours, and quiet riding there, and free libertie to depart without any moleſtation by us : they paying all ſuch duties, and charges required by law in the Countrie, as others doe . [1645]

Straies .

How diſ-poſed, Conſtable. Cryed three dayes.

IT is ordered by this Court and the Authoritie therof; that whoſoever ſhall take up any ſtraie beaſt , or finde any goods loſt wherof the owner is not known , he ſhall give notice therof to the Conſtable of the ſame Town within ſix dayes, who ſhall enter the ſame in a book and take order that it be cryed at their next Lecture day, or general Town-meeting upon three ſeverall dayes . And if it be above twenty ſhil-lings value, at the next Market or two next towns publick meetings, where no Market is within ten miles, upon pain that the partie ſo finding, and the ſaid Conſtable having ſuch notice and failing to do as is heer appointed, to forfeit either of them for ſuch de-fault one third part of the value of ſuch ſtraie, or loſt goods .

Finder neg-lecting &c. Forfeit.

And if the finder ſhall not give notice as aforeſaid within one month, or if he keep it more then three months, and ſhall not apprize it by indifferent men, and alſo re-cord it with the *Recorder* of the County Court where it is found, he ſhall then forfeit

Reſtitu: to y̆ owner.

the full value therof . And if the Owner appears within one year after ſuch publica-tion he ſhall have reſtitution of the ſame, or the value therof paying all neceſſarie charg-es, and to the Conſtable for his care and paines as one of the next Magiſtrates or the

One Magiſtr: or 3 men. No Owner appears in the year.

deputed three men of the Town ſhall adjudge . And if no Owner appear within the time prefixed the ſaid *Stray* or loſt goods ſhall be to the uſe of the finder, paying to the Conſtable ten ſhillings, or the fifth part of the value of ſuch *Straie* or goods loſt, at the finders choice .

Proviſo A with about the neck &c.

Provided that everie ſuch finder ſhall put, and keep from time to time a With or Wreath about the neck of all ſuch ſtray beaſt within one month after ſuch finding, upon penaltie of loſing all his charges that ſhall ariſe about it afterwards . Provided alſo, that

that if any Owner or other fhall take off fuch With or Wreath, or take away fuch beaft before he have difcharged according to this Order , he fhall forfeit the full value of the thing apprized as aforefaid, to the ufe of the finder, as is before expreffed . [1647]

If taken after forfeit the value.

Strangers .

IT is ordered by this Court and the Authoritie therof; that no Town or perfon fhal receive any ftranger reforting hither with intent to refide in this Jurisdiction, nor fhall allow any Lot or Habitation to any , or entertain any fuch above three weeks, except fuch perfon fhall have allowance under the hand of fome one Magiftrate , upon pain of everie Town that fhall give, or fell any Lot or Habitation to any not fo licenced fuch Fine to the Countrie as that County Court fhall impofe, not exceeding fifty pounds, nor leffe then ten pounds . And of everie perfon receiving any fuch for longer time then is heer expreffed or allowed, in fome fpecial cafes as before, or in cafe of entertainment of friends reforting from other parts of this Country in amitie with us , fhall forfeit as aforefaid, not exceeding twenty pounds, nor leffe then four pounds : and for everie month after fo offending, fhal forfeit as aforefaid not exceeding ten pounds, nor leffe then fourty fhillings . Alfo, that all Conftables fhall inform the Courts of new commers which they know to be admitted without licence, from time to time . [1637 1638 1647] *See Fugitives , Lib. com: Tryalls .*

Strangers allowed by whom, and when.

How towns & perfons finable for entertain:

monthly forfeit .
Conft: duty.

Summons .

IT is ordered, and by this Court declared; that no *Summons*, Pleading, Judgement or any kinde of proceeding in Court or courfe of juftice fhall be abated, arefted or reverfed upon any kinde of circumftantial errors or miftakes, if the perfon and the Caufe be rightly underftood and intended by the Court .

Circūftant: errors not prejudice

2 And that in all cafes where the firft *Summons* are not ferved fix dayes before the Court, and the Cafe briefly fpecified in the *Warrant* where appearance is to be made by the partie fummoned; it fhall be at his libertie whether he will appear, or not, except all Cafes that are to be handled in Courts fuddenly called upon extraordinarie occafions . And that in all cafes where there appears prefent and urgent caufe any Affiftant or Officer appointed fhall have power to make out Attachments for the firft *Summons* . Alfo, it is declared that the day of *Summons* or Attachment ferved , and the day of appearance fhall be taken inclufively as part of the fix dayes . [1641 1647] *fee Prefidents .*

Six days allowed the Defendant.

Provifo.

Where, & by whom Attachments graunted &c.

Suits, vexatious fuits .

IT is ordered and decreed, and by this Court declared; that in all Cafes where it appears to the Court that the Plaintiffe hath willingly & wittingly done wrong to the Defendant in commencing and profecuting any Action, Suit, Complaint or Indictment in his own name or in the name of others , he fhall pay treble damages to the partie greived , and be fined fourty fhillings to the Common Treafurie . [1641 1646]

Treble dam: & Fine.

Swyne .

IT is ordered by this Court, and by the Authoritie therof; that everie *Townfhip* within this Jurisdiction fhall henceforth have power, and are heerby required from time to time to make Orders for preventing all harms by fwine in corn, meadow, paftures and gardens; as alfo to impofe penalties according to their beft difcretion: and to appoint one of their Inhabitants by *Warrant* under the hands of the Select-men, or the Conftable where no Select-men are, to levie all fuch Fines and Penalties by them in that cafe impofed (if the Town neglect it) .

Town make orders.

impofe pen: levie them.

And where Towns border each upon other, whofe Orders may be various, fatisfaction fhall be made according to the Orders of that Town where the damage is done .

Orders of neigh: towns various. yoaked &c:

But if the fwine be fufficiently ringed and yoaked, as the Orders of the Town to which they belong doeth require , then where no fence is, or that it be infufficient through which the fwine come to trefpaffe, the Owner of the land or fence fhall bear all damages .

infufficient fence.

And

And if any fwine be impounded for damage done as aforefaid, & there be kept three dayes, and that no perfon will own them; then the partie damnified fhall give notice to the two next Towns (where any are within five miles compaffe) that fuch fwine are to be fold, by an out-crie, within three dayes next after fuch notice by the partie damnified; and in cafe none will buy, he fhall caufe them to be apprized by two indifferent men (one wherof fhall be the Conftable, or one chofen by him) fignified under their hands in writing, and may keep them to his own ufe. And in both cafes if the Owner fhall after appear, the overplus according to valuation as afore-faid (all damages and charges being payd) fhall forthwith be rendred to him. And if any Town fhall neglect to take order for preventing harms by fwine according to this Law, more then one month after due publication heerof, fuch town fhall forfeit to the Treafurie fourty fhillings for everie month fo neglecting, to be levied by the Marfhal by *Warrant* from the Treafurer, upon due conviction before any Court or Magiftrate, and fignified to the Treafurer from time to time. [1647]

Swine in yͤ Pound 3 days how difpofed.

Town not order: fwine forfeit 2 li.

One Magift: may hear &c:

Tile-earth .

IT is ordered by the Authoritie of this Court; that all *Tile-earth* to make fale ware fhall be digged before the firft of the ninth month, and turned over in the laft, & firft month enfuing, a month before it be wrought upon pain of forfeiting one half part of all fuch *tiles* as fhal be otherwife made, to the ufe of the Common treafurie. [1646]

Tobacco .

THIS Court finding that fince the repealing of the former Laws againft Tobacco, the fame is more abufed then before doth therfore order,

That no man fhall take any *tobacco* within twenty poles of any houfe, or fo neer as may indanger the fame, or neer any Barn, corn, or hay-cock as may occafion the fyring therof, upon pain of ten fhillings for everie fuch offence, befides full recompence of all damages done by means therof. Nor fhall any take *tobacco* in any Inne or common Victualing-houfe, except in a private room there, fo as neither the Mafter of the faid houfe nor any other Guefts there fhall take offence therat, which if any doe, then fuch perfon fhall forthwith forbear, upon pain of two fhillings fixpence for everie fuch offence. And for all Fines incurred by this Law, one half part fhall be to the Informer the other to the poor of the town where the offence is done. [1638 1647]

Tobac: where not to be taken Penal: 10 fs, recompence befides. Nor in any In except &c:

pen: 2 fs. 6 d. Penalty to the Informer & poor.

Torture .

IT is ordered, decreed, and by this Court declared; that no man fhall be forced by torture to confeffe any crime againft himfelfe or any other, unles it be in fome Capital cafe, where he is firft fully convicted by clear and fufficient evidence to be guilty. After which, if the Cafe be of that nature that it is very apparent there be other Confpirators or Confœderates with him; then he may be tortured, yet not with fuch tortures as be barbarous and inhumane.

2 And that no man fhal be beaten with above fourty ftripes for one Fact at one time. Nor fhall any man be punifhed with whipping, except he have not otherwife to anfwer the Law, unles his crime be very fhamefull, and his courfe of life vitious and *profligate*. [1641]

whipping.

Townships .

IT is ordered, decreed, and by this Court declared, that if any man fhall behave himfelfe offenfively at any Town-meeting, the reft then prefent fhall have power to fentēce him for fuch offence, fo be it the *mulct* or penalty exceed not twēty fhillings.

2 And that the Freemen of everie *Township*, and others authorized by law, fhall have power to make fuch Laws and Conftitutions as may concern the welfare of their Town. Provided they be not of a criminal but only of a prudential nature, and that their penalties exceed not twenty fhillings (as aforefaid) for one offence, and that they be not repugnant to the publick Laws and Orders of the Countrie. And if any Inhabitant fhall neglect or refufe to obferve them, they fhall have power to levie the appointed penalties by *diftreffe*.

3 Alfo that the Freemē of everie town or *Township*, with fuch other the Inhabitãts as have

offenfive behaviour at town meet: pen: not above 20 fs. by law &c:

limitation.

power to levie Penalties.

have taken the Oath of fidelitie ſhall have full power to chooſ yearly, or for leſſe time, within each *Townſhip* a convenient number of fit men to order the planting and *prudential* occaſions of that Town , according to inſtructions given them in writing .

 Provided, nothing be done by them contrary to the publick Laws and Orders of the Countrie . Provided alſo that the number of ſuch Select perſons be not aboue nine.

 4 Farther, it is ordered by the Authoritie aforeſayd , that all Towns ſhall take care from time to time to order and diſpoſe of all ſingle perſons, and In-mates within their Towns to ſervice, or otherwiſe . And if any be grieved at ſuch order or diſpoſe, they have libertie to appeal to the next County Court .

 5 *This Court taking into conſiderattion the uſefull Parts and abilities of divers Inhabitants amongſt us , which are not Freemen , which if improved to publick uſe , the affairs of this Common-wealth may be the eaſier caried an end in the ſeverall Towns of this Juriſdiction doth order, and heerby declare ;*

 That henceforth it ſhall and may be lawfull for the Freemen within any of the ſaid Towns, to make choice of ſuch Inhabitants (though non-Freemen) who have taken, or ſhall take the Oath of fidelitie to this Government to be Jurie-men , and to have their Vote in the choice of the Select-men for the town Affairs, *Aſſeſſements* of Rates, and other *Prudentials* proper to the Select-men of the ſeveral Towns . Provided ſtill that the major part of all companyes of Select-men be Free-men from time to time that ſhall make any valid Act . As alſo, where no Select-men are, to have their Vote in ordering of Schools, hearding of cattle, laying out of High-wayes and diſtributing of Lands ; any Law, Uſe or Cuſtom to the contrary notwithſtanding . Provided alſo that no non-Freeman ſhall have his Vote, untill he have attained the age of twenty one years . [1636 1641 1647] *See Eccleſiaſt: Freeman , High-wayes .*

Treaſure .

IT is ordered, decreed and by this Court declared ; that the general or publick Treaſure , or any part therof ſhall never be expended but by the appointment of a General Court , nor any Shire treaſure but by the appointment of the Freemen therof , nor any Town treaſure but by the Freemen of that *Townſhip* ; except ſmall ſums upon urgent occaſion, when the Court or the Freemen cannot direct therin , provided a juſt account be given therof . [1641]

Treſpaſſe.

IT is ordered, decreed, and by this Court declared ; that in all treſpaſſes, or damages done to any man or men, if it can be proved to be done by the meer default of him or them to whom the treſpaſſe is done , it ſhall be judged no treſpaſſe , nor any damage given for it . [1641] *See Puniſhment*

Tryalls .

WHERAS this Court is often taken up in hearing and deciding particular Caſes, between partie and partie , which more properly belong to other inferiour Courts, it is therfore ordered, and heerby declared ,

 That henceforth all Cauſes between partie and partie ſhall firſt be tryed in ſome inferiour Court . And that if the partie againſt whom the Judgment ſhall paſſe ſhall have any new evidence, or other new matter to plead, he may deſire a new *Tryall* in the ſame Court upon a *Bill* of *review* . And if juſtice ſhall not be done him upon that *Tryall* he may then come to this Court for releif . [1642] *See Cauſes, Juries .*

 2 It is ordered, and by this Court declared, that in all Actions of Law it ſhall be the libertie of the Plaintiffe and Defendant by mutuall conſent to chooſ whether they will be tryed by the Bench or a Jurie , unles it be where the Law upon juſt reaſon hath otherwiſe determined . The like libertie ſhall be graunted to all perſons in any criminal Caſes .

 3 Alſo it ſhall be in the libertie both of Plaintiffe and Defendant , & likewiſe everie delinquent to be judged by a Jurie, to challenge any of the Jurors, & if the challenge be found juſt and reaſonable , by the Bench or the reſt of the Jurie as the Challenger ſhall chooſ , it ſhall be allowed him , & *tales de circumſtantibus* impannelled in their room .

              4 Alſo

Margin notes:
Select Townſmen their power in writing &c. not above nine.

Single perſons In-mates.

Non-Freemē choſen to office in Towns.

Caution.

Caution.

Publick Treaſure

Town Treaſure.

No Cauſe between partys come firſt to ẏ Gen: Court Review

publ: liberty for tryals

& of delinq: in criminals:

Challenges

tales de cir cumſtantibus

Infants, Ide-
ots, ſtrangers,
like libertie

4 Alſo, children, Ideots, diſtracted perſons and all that are ſtrangers or new comers to our Plantation ſhall have ſuch allowances, and diſpenſations in any Caſe, whether criminal or others, as Religion and reaſon require . [1641]

Votes .

Freedom
of votes &
Caution.

liberty to
be ſilent or
neuter

where the
Preſid: will
not put to
vote.

I T is ordered, decreed and by this Court declared; that all, and everie Freeman, and others authorized by Law, called to give any Advice, Vote, Verdict or Sentence in any Court, Council or civil Aſſemblie, ſhall have full freedom to doe it according to their true judgements and conſciences , ſo it be done orderly and inoffenſively, for the manner .   And that in all caſes wherin any Freeman or other is to give his Vote be it in point of Election, making Conſtitutiõs and Orders or paſſing Sentence in any caſe of Judicature or the like , if he cannot ſee light or reaſon to give it poſitively, one way or other , he ſhall have libertie to be ſilent , and not preſſed to a determinate vote .   And farther that whenſoever any thing is to be put to vote, and Sentence to be pronounced or any other matter to be propoſed, or read in any Court or Aſſemblie, if the Preſident or Moderator ſhall refuſe to perform it, the major part of the members of that Court or Aſſemblie ſhall have power to appoint any other meet man of them to doe it .   And if there be juſt cauſe, to puniſh him that ſhould, and would not .   [1641] *See Age , Townſhips Sect.* 5.

Uſurie .

I T is ordered, decreed & by this Court declared, that no man ſhall be adjudged for the meer forbearance of any debt, above eight pounds in the hundred for one year, and not above that rate proportionably for all ſums whatſoever, *Bills* of *Exchange* excepted , neither ſhall this be a colour or countenance to allow any *uſurie* amongſt us contrary to the Law of God . [1641 1643]

Watching .

Conſt: pre-
ſent defaults
to ẙ next
Magiſtrate.
Fin, 5 ſhil:
to the uſe of
the watch.

Who are
compellable
to watch

F OR *the better keeping Watches and Wards by the Conſtables in time of peace , it is ordered by this Court and Authoritie therof;*

That everie Conſtable ſhall preſent to one of the next Magiſtrates the name of everie perſon who ſhall upon lawfull warning refuſe, or neglect to watch or ward, either in perſon, or by ſome other ſufficient for that ſervice .   And if being convented, he cannot give a juſt excuſe , ſuch Magiſtrate ſhall graunt *Warrant* to any Conſtable to levie five ſhillings of ſuch offender for everie ſuch default;   the ſame to be imployed for the uſe of the Watch of the ſame Town .   And it is the intent of the Law that everie perſon of able body (not exempted by Law) or of eſtate ſufficient to hire another ſhall be lyable to watch and ward, or to ſupplye it by ſome other when they ſhall be therunto required .   And if there be in the ſame houſe divers ſuch perſons , whether ſons, ſervants or ſojourners, they ſhall all be compellable to watch as aforeſaid .

Provided that all ſuch as keep families at their Farms , being remote from any Town, ſhall not be compellable to ſend their ſervants or ſons from their Farms to watch and ward in the Towns . [1636 1646] *See Conſtables , Militarie:*

Weights & Meaſures .

Auditor gen:
to provide a
Standard

Conſt: duty

T O *the end meaſures and weights may be one and the ſame throughout this Juriſdiction , it is ordered by the Authoritie of this Court ,*

That within one month after publication heerof the Auditor general ſhall provide upon the Countries charg ſuch weights and meaſures, of all ſorts as are heerafter expreſſed , for continuall Standards to be ſealed with the Countrie Seal ·viz: one *Buſhell*, one *Half-buſhell*, one *Peck* and one *Half-peck*, one *Ale-quart*, one *Wine-pinte* and *Half-pinte*, one *Ell* and one *Yard* :   as alſo a Set of braſſe weights to four pounds, which ſhall be after ſixteen *ounces* to the *Pound* , with fit *Skoals* and *Steel-beams* to weigh and trye withall .

2 And it is farther ordered by the Authortie aforeſaid, that the Conſtable of everie Town within this Juriſdiction ſhall within three months after publication heerof provide upon the Towns charge all ſuch *Weights*, at the leaſt of *Lead*, or ſuch like; and alſo ſufficient *Meaſures* as are above expreſſed , tryed and ſized by the Countries Standards

Standards, and ſealed by the ſayd Auditor general, or his Deputie in his preſence (which ſhall be kept and uſed only for Standards for their ſeverall towns) who is heerby authorized to doe the ſame; for which he ſhall receive from the Conſtable of each town, two pence for everie *weight* and *meaſure* ſo proved, ſized and ſealed . And the ſaid Conſtables of everie town ſhall commit theſe *weights* and *meaſures* unto the cuſtodie of the Select-men of their towns, for the time being, who with the ſaid Conſtable are heerby injoyned to chooſ out of their company one able man to be the Sealer of ſuch things for their town from time to time, and till another be choſen : which man, ſo choſen, they ſhall preſent to the next County Court there to be ſworn to the faithfull diſcharge of his duty, who ſhall have power to ſend forth his *Warrants* by the Conſtables to all the Inhabitants of their town to bring in all ſuch *meaſures* and *weights* as they make any uſe of, in the ſecond month from year to year, at ſuch time and place as he ſhall appoint, and make return to the Sealer in writing of all perſons ſo ſummoned that then and there all ſuch *weights* and *meaſures* may be proved and ſealed with the towns Seal (ſuch as in the Order for town cattle) provided by the Conſtable of each towns charge; who ſhall have for everie *weight* and *meaſure* ſo ſealed, one pennie from the Owners therof at the firſt ſealing .

And all ſuch *meaſures* and *weights* as cannot be brought to their juſt Standard he ſhall deface, or deſtroy; and after the firſt ſealing ſhall have nothing ſo long as they continue juſt with the Standard . And that none may neglect their duty therin, it is farther ordered by the Authoritie aforeſaid, that if any Conſtable, Select-men or Sealer doe not execute this Order, as to everie of them appertains, they ſhall forfeit to the common Treaſurie fourty ſhillings for everie ſuch neglect the ſpace of one month : and alſo that everie perſon neglecting to bring in their *weights* and *meaſures* at the time and place appointed, they ſhall pay three ſhillings four pence for everie ſuch default, one half part wherof ſhall be to the Sealer, and the other half to the common Treaſurie, which the Sealer ſhall have power to levie by *diſtreſſe* from time to time . [1647]

Wharfage .

IT is ordered by this Court and the Authoritie therof; that theſe Orders ſhall be obſerved by all ſuch as ſhall bring goods to any *Wharf*, and theſe rates following be allowed; firſt, for wood by the tun three pence, for timber by the tun four pence, for pipeſtaves by the thouſand nine pence, for boards by the thouſand ſix pence. For Merchants goods, whether in cask or otherwiſe, by the tun ſix pence; for drie fiſh by the *Quintall* one pennie, for corn by the quarter one pennie and a half pennie, for great cattle by the head two pence, for Goats, Swine or other ſmall cattle, except ſuch as are ſucking upon the dams, by the head a half-pennie: for hay, ſtraw and all ſuch combuſtable goods by the load ſix pence . For ſtones by the tun one pennie, for cotten wool by the bag two pence, for ſugar by the cheſt three pence . Provided that *Wharfage* be taken only where the *Wharfs* are made and maintained . And that wood, ſtone and weighty goods ſhall be ſet up an end, or layd ſeven foot from the ſide of the *Wharf*, upon penalty of double *Wharfage*, and ſo for other goods . And that no goods lye upon the *Wharf* above fourtie eight hours, without farther agreement with the *Wharfinger*: and that it ſhall be lawful for the *Wharfinger* to take according to theſe rates out of the goods that are landed, except they be ſatified otherwiſe .

2 And it is farther ordered, that none ſhall caſt an Anker, Graplin or Killack within, or neer the Cove, where it may indanger any other veſſels, upon penaltie of ten ſhillings half to the Countrie, half to the *Wharfinger* beſides paying all damages .

3 And that it ſhall not be lawfull for any perſon to caſt any dung, draught, dirt, or any thing to fill up the Cove, or to annoy the neighbours, upon penaltie of fourty ſhillings, the one half to the Countrie, and the other half to the *Wharfinger* . [1647]

Wills inteſtate .

IT is ordered, and by this Court declared; that when Parents dye *inteſtate*, the eldeſt ſon ſhall have a double portion of his whole eſtate reall, and perſonall unles the General Court upon juſt cauſe alledged ſhall judge otherwiſe . And when Parents

H   dye

(marginal notes:)
his Fee, two pence.

Conſt: and Select-men appoint a Sealer. to be ſworn ẙ next County Court, his power & duty.

his Fee, one pennie.

What meaſ: deſtroyed. No Fees.

Rates for wharfage.

Wharfs made & maintain: orderly placing goods.

caſt: Ankers, pen: 10 ſs & damages,

caſt: dung &c: penal: 40 ſs.

dye *inteſtate* having no Heirs males of their bodyes, their daughters ſhall inherit as co-partners, unles the General Court upon juſt reaſon ſhall judge otherwiſe. [1641]

Witneſſes .

I T is ordered, decreed, and by this Court declared, that no man ſhall be put to death without the teſtimonie of two or three *witneſſes*, or that which is equivalent therunto . [1641]

Teſtimonie taken before one Magiſt:

2 And it is ordered by this Court and the Authoritie therof, that any one Magiſtrate, or Commiſſioner authorized therunto by the General Court may take the Teſtimonie of any perſon of fourteen years of age , or above, of ſound underſtanding and reputation, in any Caſe civil or criminal;   and ſhall keep the ſame in his own hands till the Court, or deliver it to the Recorder, publick Notarie or Clerk of the writs to be recorded, that ſo nothing may be altered in it.   Provided, that where any ſuch *witneſſe* ſhall have his abode within ten miles of the Court, and there living and not diſabled by ſicknes, or o-ther infirmitie, the ſaid Teſtimonie ſo taken out of Court ſhall not be received, or made uſe of in the Court, except the *witnes* be alſo preſent to be farther examined about it .   Provided alſo, that in all capital caſes all *witneſſes* ſhall be preſent whereſoever they dwell.

how ordered:

Where wit-neſſes to ap pear in perſon.

Capital caſes.

3 And it is farther ordered by the Authoritie aforeſaid, that any perſon ſummoned to appear as a *witnes* in any civil Court between partie and partie, ſhall not be compellable to travell to any Court or place where he is to give his Teſtimonie, except he who ſhall ſo ſummon him ſhall lay down or give him ſatisfaction for his travell and expences, out-ward and home-ward;   and for ſuch time as he ſhall ſpend in attendance in ſuch caſe when he is at ſuch Court or place, the Court ſhall award due recompence .   And it is ordered that two ſhillings a day ſhall be accounted due ſatisfaction to any *Witnes* for travell and expences :   and that when the *Witnes* dwelleth within three miles, and is not at charge to paſſe over any other Ferrie then betwixt *Charlſtown* and *Boſton* then one ſhilling ſix pence *per diem* ſhall be accounted ſufficient .   And if any *Witnes* after ſuch payment or ſatisfaction ſhall fail to appear to give his Teſtimonie he ſhall be ly-able to pay the parties damages upon an action of the *Caſe* .   And all *Witneſſes* in crimi-nal caſes ſhall have ſuitable ſatisfaction, payd by the Treaſurer upon *Warrant* from the Court or Judge before whom the caſe is tryed .   And for a general rule to be obſerv-ed in all criminal cauſes, both where the Fines are put *in certain*, and alſo where they are otherwiſe, it is farther ordered by the Authoritie aforeſayd, that the charges of *Witneſſes* in all ſuch caſes ſhall be borne by the parties delinquent, and ſhall be added to the Fines impoſed;   that ſo the Treaſurer having upon *Warrant* from the Court or other Judge ſatisfied ſuch *Witneſſes*, it may be repayd him with the Fine: that ſo the *Wit-neſſes* may be timely ſatisfied, and the countrie not damnified . [1647]

charges of witneſſes in civil caſes to be layd down

Allowance to witneſſes by the day.

Witnes not appearing pay damages,

witnes in cri-minal caſes payd by the Treaſurer, levied of ỹ delinquents

Wolves .

W HERAS *great loſſe & damage doth befall this Common-wealth by reaſon of* Wolves *which deſtroy great numbers of our cattle notwithſtanding proviſion formerly made by this Court for ſuppreſſing of them: therfore for the better incouragement of any to ſet about a work of ſo great concernment it is ordered by this Court and Authoritie therof*;

That any perſon either Engliſh or Indian that ſhall kill any *wolfe* or *wolves* within ten miles of any Plantation in this Juriſdiction, ſhall have for everie *wolfe* by him or them ſo killed ten ſhillings payd out of the Treaſurie of the Countrie .   Provided that due proof be made therof unto the Plantation next adjoyning where ſuch *wolfe* or *wolves* were killed: and alſo they bring a *Certificat* under ſome Magiſtrates hand, or the Conſtable of that place unto the Treaſurer .   Provided alſo that this Order doth in-tend only ſuch Plantations as do contribute with us to publick charges , and for ſuch Plantations upon the river of *Piſcataway* that do not joyn with us to carie on publick charges they ſhall make payment upon their own charge . [1645]

Wood .

F OR *the avoyding of injuries by carts and boats, to ſellers and buyers of wood, it is or-dered by this Court and the Authoritie therof,*

That

That where wood is brought to any town or houfe, by boat, it fhall be thus accounted and affized. A boat of four tuns fhall be accounted three loads; twelve tun nine loads, twenty tun fifteen loads. Six tun four load and half, fourteen tun ten load and half, twenty-four tun eighteen load. Eight tun fix load, fixteen tun twelve load, twenty eight tun twenty one load. Ten tun feven load and half, eighteen tun thirteen load and half; thirty tun twenty two load and half. Except fuch wood as fhall be fold by the *Cord*, which is, and is heerby declared to be eight foot in length, four foot in height, and four foot broad. [1646 1647]

Workmen.

B ECAUSE *the harveft of hay, corn, hemp and flax comes ufually fo neer together that much loffe can hardly be avoyded, it is therefore ordered by the Authoritie of this Court;*

That the Conftables of everie town, upon requeft made to them, fhal require any artificers or handy-crafts-men meet to labour, to work by the day for their neighbours in mowing, reaping of corn and inning therof. Provided that thofe men whom they work for fhall duly pay them for their work. And that if any perfon fo required fhall refufe, or the Conftable negleft his Office heerin, they fhall each of them pay to the ufe of the poor of the town double fo much as fuch dayes work comes unto. Provided no artificer or handy-crafts-man fhall be compelled to work as aforefaid, for others, whiles he is neceffarily attending on the like bufines of his own. [1646]

Wrecks of the fea.

I T is ordered, decreed and by this Court declared; that if any fhips or other veffels, be it freind or enemie, fhall fuffer fhip-wreck upon our Coafts, there fhall be no violence or wrong offered to their perfons, or goods; but their perfons fhall be harboured and releived, and their goods preferved in fafety, till Authoritie may be certified, and fhall take farther order therin. Alfo, any Whale, or fuch like great fifh, caft upon any fhore fhall be fafely kept, or improved where it cannot be kept, by the town or other proprietor of the land; till the General Court fhall fet order for the fame. [1641 1647]

Prefidents and Forms of things frequently ufed.

T O (*IB*) Carpenter, of (*D*). You are required to appear at the next Court, holden at (*B*) on the   day of the   month next enfuing; to anfwer the complaint of (*N C*) for with-holding a debt of   due upon a *Bond* or *Bill*: or for two heifers &c: fold you by him, or for work, or for a trefpaffe done him in his corn or hay, by your cattle, or for a flaunder you have done him in his name, or for ftriking him, or the like, and heerof you are not to fail at your peril. Dated the   day of the   month 1641. — *Summons.*

T O the Marfhal or Conftable of (*B*) or to their Deputie. You are required to attach the body and goods of (*WF*) and to take *Bond* of him, to the value of   with fufficient Suertie or Suerties for his appearance at the next Court, holden at (*S*) on the   day of the   month; then, and there to anfwer to the complaint of (*T M*) for &c: *as before*. And fo make a true return therof under your hand. Dated the   day &c: *By the Court.*   *R. F.* — *Attachment.*

K NOW all men by thefe prefents, that wee (*AB*) of (*D*) Yeoman, and (*C C*) of the fame, Carpenter, doe binde our felves, our Heirs and Executors to (*R P*) Marfhal, or *M O* Conftable of *D* aforefaid, in   pounds; upon condition that the   faid — *Bond for appearance*

Replevin

said *A B* fhall perfonally appear at the next Court, at *S* to anfwer *L M* in an Action of   And to abide the order of the Court therin, & not to depart without licence.

TO the Marfhal or Conftable of   You are required to *replevie* three heifers of *T P* now diftreined or impounded by *A B*, and to deliver them to the faid *T P*. Provided he give *Bond* to the value of   with fufficient Suertie or Suerties to profecute his *Replevin* at the next Court, holden at (*B*) and fo from Court to Court till the Caufe be ended, and to pay fuch cofts and damages as the faid (*A B*) fhall by law recover againft him; and fo make a true return therof under your hand. Dated &c:

By the Court.

R. F.

Commiffio-
ners for the
united
Colonies.

their power

WHERAS upon ferious confideration, wee have concluded a confœderacie with the englifh Colonies of *New-Plimouth , Connecticot* and *New-Haven ,* as the bond of nature, reafon, Religion and refpect to our Nation doth require:

Wee have this Court chofen our truftie and well-beloved freinds (*S B*) and (*W H*) for this Colonie, for a full and compleat year, as any occafions and exigents may require and particularly for the next Meeting at (*B*).   And do inveft them with full power and authoritie to treat, and conclude of all things, according to the true tenour and meaning of the Articles of confœderation of the united Colonies, concluded at *Bofton* the ninth day of the third month 1643.

Oath of
fidelitie.

I (*A B*) being by Gods providence an Inhabitant within the Jurisdiction of this Common-wealth, doe freely and fincerly acknowledge my felfe to be fubject to the Government therof.   And doe heer fwear by the great and dreadfull Name of the Ever-living God, that I will be true and faithfull to the fame, and will accordingly yeild affiftance therunto, with my perfon and eftate, as in equitie I am bound: and will alfo truly indeavour to maintein and preferve all the Liberties & Priviledges therof, fubmitting my felf unto the wholfom Laws made, & eftablifhed by the fame.   And farther, that I will not plot or practice any evil againft it, or confent to any that fhall fo doe: but will timely difcover and reveal the fame to lawfull Authoritie now heer eftablifhed, for the fpeedy preventing therof.   So help me God in our Lord Jefus Chrift.

Freemans
Oath.

I (*A B*) being by Gods providence an Inhabitant within the Jurisdiction of this Common-wealth, and now to be made free;   doe heer freely acknowledge my felf to be fubject to the Government therof: and therfore do heer fwear by the great and dreadfull Name of the Ever-living God, that I will be true and faithfull to the fame, & will accordingly yeild affiftance & fupport therunto, with my perfon and eftate, as in equitie I am bound, and will alfo truly indeavour to maintein & preferve all the Liberties and Priviledges therof, fubmitting my felf unto the wholfom Laws made and eftablifhed by the fame.   And farther, that I will not plot or practice any evil againft it, or confent to any that fhall fo doe;   but will timely difcover & reveal the fame to lawfull authoritie now heer eftablifhed, for the fpeedy prevention therof.

Moreover, I do folemnly binde my felf in the fight of God, that when I fhall be called to give my voice touching any fuch matter of this State, wherin Free-men are to deal;   I will give my vote and *fuffrage* as I fhall in mine own confcience judge beft to conduce and tend to the publick weal of the Body, without refpect of perfons, or favour of any man.   So help me God &c:

Governours
Oath.

WHERAS you (*J W*) are chofen to the place of a Governour over this Jurisdiction, for this year, and till a new be chofen & fworn: you do heer fwear by the Living God, that you will in all things concerning your place, according to your beft power and skill carie and demean your felf for the faid time of your Government, according to the Laws of God, & for the advancement of his Gofpell, the Laws of this land, and the good of the people of this Jurisdiction.   You fhall doe juftice to all men without partialitie, as much as in you lyeth: you fhall not exceed the limitations of a Governour in your place.   So help you God &c:

Deputie
Gover:

WHERAS you (*T D*) are chofen to the place of the Deputie-Governour &c: *as in the Governours Oath , mutatis mutandis .*

Wheras

W HERAS you (*R B*) are chofen to the place of *Affiftant* over this Jurifdiction, for this year, and till new be chofen and fworn : you doe heer fwear by the Living God, that you will trulie indeavour according to your beft skill, to carie and de-mean your felf in your place, for the faid time, according to the Laws of God & of this land, for the advancement of the Gofpell & the good of the people of this Jurifdictiõ. You fhall difpenfe juftice equallie and impartiallie, according to your beft skill in all ca-fes wherin you fhall act by vertue of your place . You fhall not wittinglie & willing-lie exceed the limitations of your place . And all this to be underftood, during your abode in this Jurifdiction . So help you God in our Lord Jefus Chrift .   *Affiftants*

W HERAS you (*J E*) have been chofen to the Office of Sergeant Major General, of all the militarie Forces of this Jurifdiction, for this prefent year : You doe heer fwear by the Ever-living God, that by your beft skill and abilitie you will faithfullie difcharge the truft committed to you, according to the tenour and purport of the Com-miffion given you by this Court . So help you God &c: *Major General.*

I (*R R*) beng chofen *Treafurer* for the Jurifdiction of the *Maffachufets*, for this year, and untill a new be chofen; doe promife to give out *Warrants* with all convenient diligence, for collecting all fuch fums of monie as by any Court, or other-wife have been, or fhall be appointed, and to pay out the fame, by fuch fums and in fuch manner as I fhall be lawfullie appointed by this Court, if I fhall have it in my hands of the Common Treafurie . And will return the names of fuch Conftables as fhall be failing in their Office, in not collecting and bringing in to mee fuch fums as I fhall give *Warrant* for . And will render a true account of all things concerning my faid Office, when by the General Court I fhall be called thereto . So help me God in our Lord Jefus Chrift .   *Treafurer*

Y Ou (*W A*) heer fwear by the Name of the Living God; that in the Office of a *Publick Notarie*, to which you have been chofen, you fhall demean your felfe diligentlie and faithfullie according to the dutie of your Office . And in all writings, in-ftrumẽts & articles that you are to give teftimonie unto, when you fhall be required, you fhall perform the fame trulie and finceerlie according to the nature therof, without delay or *covin*. And you fhall enter, and keep a true Regifter of all fuch things as belong to your Office . So help &c: *Publick Notarie.*

Y Ou (*E M*) fhall diligentlie, faithfullie, and with what fpeed you may, collect and gather up all fuch Fines, and fums of monie, in fuch goods as you can finde, of everie perfon for which you fhall have *Warrant* fo to do by the Treafurer for the time being . And with like faithfullnes, fpeed and diligence levie the goods of everie perfon for which you fhall have *Warrant* fo to doe, by vertue of any *Execution* graunted by the Secretarie, or other Clerk authorized therunto, for the time being . And the fame goods fo collected or levied, you fhall with all convenient fpeed deliver in to the Trea-furer, or the perfons to whom the fame fhall belong . And you fhall with like care & faithfullnes, ferve all *Attachments* directed to you, which fhall come to your hands; & return the fame to the Court where they are returnable, at the times of the return therof.   *Marfhal.*

And you fhall perform, doe and execute all fuch lawfull commands, directiõs and warrants, as by lawfull Authoritie heer eftablifhed fhall be committed to your care & charge, according to your Office . All thefe things in the prefence of the Living God you binde your felfe unto, by this your Oath to perform, during all the time you continue in your Office, without favour, fear, or partialitie of any perfon . (And if you meet with anie cafe of dificultie which you cannot refolve by your felfe, you may fuf-pend till you may have advice from Authoritie) So help &c:

Y Ou (*N D*) do fwear by the Living God, that you will well and trulie ferve this Common-wealth in the Office of *Auditor General*, wherunto you have been chofen; fo long as you fhall continue in the fame . You fhall keep a true account of all things committed to your charge . You fhall not omit or delay without juft oc-cafion, to examin, figne and difpatch all accounts and bills which fhall be brought to you for that end, without taking any Fee or reward for the fame, other then the   *Auditor General.*

H 3   General

General Court hath allowed, or fhall allow :   and fhall give a true account of all your
bufines , when you fhall be thereto required by the faid Court . So help you God &c:

Affociates.
Y OU (*M N*) being chofen Affociate for the Court, for this year, and till new be
chofen or other order taken , doe heer fwear, that you will doe equal right and
juftice in all cafes that fhall come before you, after your beft skill and knowledge , according to the laws heer eftablifhed . So help you God &c:

Wherefoever any three men are deputed to end fmall Caufes, the Conftable of the place with-
in one month after, fhall return their names to the next Magiftrate, who fhall give Sum-
mons for them forthwith to appear before him; who fhall adminifter to them this Oath:

Three men.
Y Ou (*A B*) being chofen & appointed to end fmall Caufes, not exceeding fourty
fhillings value, according to the laws of this Jurisdiction, for this year enfuing,
doe heer fwear by the Living God that without favour or affection , according to your
beft light, you will true Judgement give and make, in all the Caufes that come before
you . So help you God &c:

Grand
Iurie.
Y Ou fwear by the Living God, that you will diligently inquire, & faithfully prefent to this Court, whatfoever you know to be a breach of any law eftablifhed
in this Jurisdiction according to the minde of God ; and whatfoever criminal offences
yon apprehend fit to be heer prefented , uules fome neceffarie and religious tye of confcience, truly grounded upon the word of God binde you to fecrefie. And whatfoever
fhall be legally committed by this Court to your judgement, you will return a true and
juft Verdict therin, according to the evidence given you, and the laws eftablifhed a-
mongft us . So help you God &c:

Pettie
Iurie.
Y Ou fwear by the Living God, that in the Caufe or Caufes now legally to be
committed to you by this Court, you will true triall make, and juft verdict
give therin , according to the evidence given you, and the laws of this Jurisdiction . So
help you God &c:

Life &
death.
Y Ou doe fwear by the great Name of Almightie God, that you will well & truly trie, and true deliverance make of fuch prifoners at the *Bar* as you fhall have
in charge, according to your evidence . So help you God &c:

Witneffes.
Y Ou fwear by the Living God , that the evidence you fhall give to this Court,
concerning the Caufe now in queftion, fhall be the truth, the whole truth, and
nothing but the truth . So help you God &c:

Untimely
death.
Y Ou fwear by the Living God, that you will truly prefent the caufe and the manner of the death of (*J B*) according to evidence , or the light of your knowledge and confcience. So help you God &c:

The form of the Oath to be adminiftred to the Sergeant Majors of the feverall Regiments,
and fo, mutatis mutandis, *to the other militarie Officers* .

Sergeant
Major &
other chief
Officers.
W Heras you (*R S*) have been chofen to the Office of Sergeant Major, of the Regiment in the Countie of *M.* for this prefent year, and untill another be chofen
in your place; You doe heer fwear by the Living God, that by your beft skill & abilitie you will faithfully difcharge the truft committed to you, according to fuch commands and directions as you fhall from time to time upon all occafions receive from the
Sergeant Major General , by vertue of his Commiffion from the Court, and according
to the Laws and Orders by this Court made and eftablifhed in this behalf . So help you
God &c:

Clerk of
the Band.
Y Ou (*R. B*) fwear trulie to perform the Office of a Clerk of a trained Band, to the
utmoft of your abilitie, or indeavours , according to the particulars fpecified
[and peculiar to your office] in the militarie Laws . So help &c:

Commiffio:
of martial
difciplin
Y Ou fhall faithfullie indeavour with all good confcience, to difcharge this truft
committed to yon, as you fhall apprehend to conduce moft to the fafetie of this
Common-wealth .   You fhall not by any finifter devices , or for any partial
refpects , or private ends doe any thing to the hindrance of the effects of any good
and feafonable Counfels .   You fhall appoint or remove no Officer by anie
partialitie, or for perfonal refpects , or other prejudice :   but according to the
merit

merit of the perfons in your apprehentions . You fhall faithfully indeavour to fee that martial difciplin may be ftrictly upholden , not eafing or burthening any , otherwife then you fhall judge to be juft and equal . You fhall ufe your power over mens lives, as the laft and only means which in your beft apprehentions fhall be moft for the pub-lick fafety in fuch cafe . So help you God in our Lord Jefus Chrift .

W HERAS you (*E G*) are chofen Conftable within the Town of (*C*), for one year now following , and untill other be fworn in the place: you doe heer fwear by the Name of Almighty God , that you will carefully intend the prefervation of the peace , the difcovery and preventing all attempts againft the fame . You fhall duly execute all *Warrants* which fhall be fent unto you from lawfull Authoritie heer efta-blifhed , & fhall faithfully execute all fuch Orders of Court as are committed to your care : and in all thefe things you fhall deal ferioufly and faithfully while you fhall be in office, without any finifter refpects of favour or difpleafure , So help you God &c: *Conftable.*

W HERAS you (*J G*) are chofen an Officer for the fearching and fealing of lea-ther within the Town where you now dwell , for the fpace of a year , and till another be chofen and fworn in your room . You do heer fwear by the Ever-liv-ing God, that you will carefully and duly attend the execution of your faid Office , with all faithfullnes for the good of the Common-wealth , according to the true intent of the Laws in fuch cafe provided . So help you God &c: *Leather Sealer.*

Y OU (*C D*) heer fwear by the Living God that you will from time to time faith-fully execute your Office of *Clerk of the Market* , in the limits whereto you are appointed , for this enfuing year, and till another be chofen and fworn in your place : and that you will doe therin impartially, according to the Laws heer eftab-lifhed , in all things to which your Office hath relation . So help you God &c: *Clerk of Market.*

Y OU (*S S*) doe heer fwear by the Ever-living God , that you will to your power faithfully execute the Office of a *Searcher* for this year enfuing , and till another be chofen and fworn in your place , concerning all goods prohibited ; and in fpecial, for *Gun-powder*, *Shot, Lead and Amunition* : and that you will diligently fearch all veffels, carriages and perfons that you fhall know, fufpect, or be informed are about to tranfport, or carie the fame out of this Jurisdiction contrary to Law . And that you will impartially feiz, take, and keep the fame in your own cuftodie : one half part wherof fhall be for your fervice in the faid Place; the other you fhall forthwith deliver to the Treafurer . All which goods fo feized and difpofed , you fhall certifie under your hand to the Auditor-general within one month from time to time . So help you God &c: *Searcher.*

W HERAS you (*T. D.*) are chofen *Apprizers of* fuch *lands* or goods as are now to be prefented to you , you doe heer fwear by the Living God , that all par-tialitie, prejudice and other finifter refpects layd afide , you fhall apprize the fame, and everie part therof, according to the true and juft value therof at this prefent, by common account, by your beft judgement and confcience . So help you God &c: *Apprizers*

W HERAS you (*J. B.*) are chofen to be *Viewers of Pipe-ftaves* within the Town of (*B*) you doe heer fwear by the Ever-living God , that at all convenient times while you fhall be in place, when you fhall be required to execute your Office , you fhall diligently attend the fame; and fhall faithfully without any finifter refpects, try and fort all *Pipe-ftaves* prefented to you, and make a true entrie therof according to law . So help you God in our Lord Jefus Chrift . *Viewers of Pipeftaves.*

FINIS

SEVEN HUNDRED AND FIFTY COPIES OF THIS REVISED EDITION OF

The Laws and Liberties of Massachusetts

WERE PRINTED ON FINCH VANILLA OPAQUE TEXT AT

THE STINEHOUR PRESS, LUNENBURG, VERMONT.

THE TYPE FOR THE FRONT MATTER WAS SET

IN ADOBE CASLON, A REDRAWN AND

DIGITIZED VERSION OF THE

MONOTYPE CASLON

USED IN THE 1929

EDITION.

❦

BOOKS BOUND BY ACME BOOKBINDING,

CHARLESTOWN, MASSACHUSETTS.